SWITCHING TRACKS

*Advancing Through
Five Crucial Phases
of Your Career*

JOHN BRADLEY

with Dave and Neta Jackson

Fleming H. Revell
A Division of Baker Book House Co
Grand Rapids, Michigan 49516

©1994 by John D. Bradley with Dave and Neta Jackson

Published by Fleming H. Revell
a division of Baker Book House Company
P.O. Box 6287, Grand Rapids, MI 49516-6287

Printed in the United States of America

Library of Congress Cataloging-in-Publication Data

Bradley, John D. (John David), 1947–
    Switching tracks : advancing through five crucial phases of your career / John Bradley, with Dave and Neta Jackson.
       p.   cm.
    ISBN 0-8007-5527-8
    1. Career development—Case studies. I. Jackson, Dave. II. Jackson, Neta. III. Title.
    HF5381.B6378   1994
    650.14—dc20   94-17582

SWITCHING TRACKS

To
Carolyn Hagenbaugh,
Tom Lyman, Jim Hamilton, and Don and Emily Doot,
faithful coworkers who have mastered
their crafts

Contents

Introduction

At age forty-two, you have nailed a midlevel management position with a high-tech computer firm. A few of your ideas have found their way into new systems, resulting in some nice bonuses and regular promotions. Rumor has it that you're on a short list for a senior management position. But the pressure is on. It's the men and women who are married to their jobs, put in long hours, and are willing to represent the company in Washington, D.C., or London or Tokyo who rise through the ranks, get the best positions, and pull down the big salaries. Part of you is excited about the bright future that seems to be opening up in front of you . . . but part of you is worried. You have two teenagers in school, one of whom is on probation for being caught with marijuana in his locker, and your younger child seems to have changed overnight into a sullen, rebellious eighth grader. You know that you should be spending more time at home—not less—giving attention to the kids. But refusing a promotion could be career suicide. If you changed jobs now, would you lose your professional edge? What kind of job could make use of your skills and experience, and leave room for your family, too?

You're thirty years old, a teacher in an urban high school. When you first chose teaching as a career, you were filled with enthusiasm for imparting knowledge to thirsty young minds. You believed—and still do—that education is the key to success, the ladder out of poverty and hopelessness, the magic carpet to exploring an exciting and ever-expanding world. But after seven short years, you already feel burned out. The reality of the classroom is not what you anticipated. You never counted on having to spend the majority of your time dealing with uncooperative parents, or acting as a social worker to kids stressed out by drugs, gang pressure, or sexual activity. You just wanted to teach, to teach kids who wanted to learn. You feel like quitting—but teaching is what you were trained for. What are you going to do?

You're a forty-eight-year-old project director with a large book-publishing firm. You majored in journalism and have a master's degree in communication. You've been with the company for almost twenty years, have risen from assistant editor to editor to managing editor to project director—with commensurate salary raises and benefits. You're well respected among your colleagues, you enjoy the occasional business trips to meet with authors and the annual publishing planning meeting (in the Colorado Rockies!), and you appreciate the job security. But recently you've been feeling dissatisfied. You realize that in rising through the ranks in the company, you have moved farther and farther away from what you really enjoy: hands-on writing and editing. Now all your time is spent with flow charts, delegating responsibilities, and supervising employees—administration. But giving up a secure job in the publishing field and opting for the uncertainties of a writer's life seem crazy at this stage of your life.

You're a thirty-five-year-old homemaker. You've really enjoyed your years at home with your three children, but the youngest one is now in school all day and you feel a little guilty about not having a job. Your husband has never pressured you to work outside the home, but the furniture is threadbare and vacations have been limited to a week-long camping trip each summer. You have an undergraduate degree in business administration, and you're toying with the idea of going back to school to brush up on your skills. But after twelve years of being in the people-development business (i.e., raising well-rounded kids), you're not so sure you could stand an eight-to-five desk job. Still, all your friends have jobs or careers, and you feel slightly useless and antiquated.

Making a Difference

Are you still searching for what you're going to be when you grow up . . . even if you are thirty or fifty? If so, you are not alone. Since 1969, when I began assisting people in midcareer assessment and job transitions, I have noted that we all yearn down deep in our hearts to make a difference so that when our lives are over we can look back and say, "I accomplished something that made it worth it all." I think each of us secretly desires to rise to the level of master craftsperson with some talent or trade.

Becoming a master craftsperson involves more than obtaining an academic degree or occupational title such as president. Rather, it is the creative mastery of some particular task, whether carpentry or music, ministry or banking, computing or personnel managing, teaching or homemaking. Because of this desire to excel, many of us are still searching for "what I'm going to be when I grow up."

At this point you may be exasperated from having tried many paths that you thought would lead to success but only brought you to dead ends. Or you may be just getting started in your search. In either case, the desire for purpose and achievement is still strong. This book is designed to fuel the flame of that desire and show you that you are gifted with inherent aptitudes that—when properly focused—can lead to excellence.

Moments of Truth

From time to time in life, each of us faces a challenge that tells us whether we've truly mastered a task in our life quest. For me, one of those tests came during a business seminar I led in 1986. It was a two-day training event for corporate human-resource directors and company presidents that was in Minneapolis.

Prior to that time, my work had involved counseling individuals in midcareer transition, but now we were launching something new. Although my company had pilot-tested our material for about a year in the corporate sector, this seminar represented a special challenge because in the audience was Dr. Michael O'Connor, a nationally recognized expert in employee job performance assessment. I usually enjoy challenges, but in the back of my mind was the anxious question, "What does he think of all this?" I searched for clues in his every expression and movement.

At the end of the seminar, I invited evaluative comments. As expected, some people said kind things; others had questions. Then, when it appeared that everyone had spoken, our esteemed visitor raised his hand and began with a statement: "Some of you may not realize it, but I am a professional in this field and am well versed in all the related research."

My heart began to pound. I glanced over to our staff and saw their eyes widen. Everything was on the line. There were bank executives, corporate human resource managers, and company presidents sitting in the room, and they were all about to hear what this expert thought of our material.

Dr. O'Connor continued: "This has been one of the most delightful training sessions in which I have participated. Furthermore, I believe that the concept of natural talents is the missing link in assessing human potential, one that we as professionals have been looking for for a long time. I think this material is three to five years ahead of our time, and I heartily endorse and encourage its use."

That statement took no more than a minute to make, but his generous affirmation helped me discover where I stood in the field of aptitude assessment and midcareer counseling. Needless to say, the rest of our staff also acknowledged the significance of that moment.

Each of us longs for those moments when our contributions to life are measured and found worthy in ways we respect and know are genuine. They need not involve public praise, glory, or popular success. They can also be quiet reflections regarding the accomplishment of a goal. Indeed, public accolades can prove hollow if they supplant authentic evaluation of whether we are becoming master craftspersons in what we do.

I believe that the clear understanding of one's talent strengths is one of the most significant factors in achieving that noteworthy, lifetime contribution. Many people go through several assessments and adjustments in search of the right occupation and still miss the very important appraisal of their talents. Without that foundation, a well-intended search can lead to disappointment at age fifty and beyond, or worse—bitterness and a sense of failure.

The Times of Our Lives

As I have observed people in transition for the last twenty years, I believe most people pass through five phases of adult life. During each phase they naturally encounter several points where self-evaluation and adjustment can take place. Whether or not people avail themselves of these opportunities has a great deal to do with how well adjusted and fulfilled they are. To describe why and how some people become master craftspersons while others do not, I have chosen the format of relating the life stories of five characters (beginning in chapter 3) as they navigate through their adult lives. Their stories illustrate how the decisions we make in life contribute to either fulfillment or derailment of our desire to make a difference in life and to achieve excellence.

The characters themselves are composites of clients with whom I have worked during twenty years of career-assessment and job-transition counseling. From this experience I have identified five phases of adult life through which we all pass. The choices we make at each of these critical decision points can make the next phase of life either more fulfilling or more difficult. As an adult, you are in one of these five phases. To assess your current experience and level of personal satisfaction, however, you must go back to phase one, when you were leaving adolescence and entering adulthood, and evaluate the presuppositions that launched you in the life direction you have taken. To make progress in the future, you must distinguish between the correct and the mythical assumptions that drive you. If you operate on faulty presuppositions, you need to correct those to make progress in the future.

The following is a brief overview of each phase. Please note that the ages I have assigned to each phase are approximate and therefore there will be an overlap in ages between each phase.

Phase 1: Passionate Pursuits

I have found that most people start their adult lives with a phase of "passionate pursuits" (ages twenty to thirty). As young adults who desire to make a difference with our lives, we set our minds to pursuing our passions with seemingly inexhaustible energy. Whether it is medicine or parenthood, religion or revolution, we have discovered—and have been told—that more energy produces better results. So, with the encouragement of parents and relatives and other mentors, we go to college or get other training and confront the world with zeal and enthusiasm. That zeal and enthusiasm continues to be one of the most important components in our success or failure until the age of thirty. In fact, it is so important that we seldom look at other factors. If success eludes us, we just try harder. The key characteristics of this phase are optimism and almost unlimited energy to pursue a dream or career goal.

Phase 2: Evaluating the Results

Around age thirty or shortly thereafter, however, we usually move into a phase of "evaluating the results." Perhaps it is triggered by the grind of our work, but at this point we begin wondering, "Am I going down the right path? Is it working out? Is this really what I want to be or do for the rest of my life?"

Surprisingly, it is a physiological factor that underlies the need for this evaluation. Physicians tell us that at about age thirty, our bodies peak, and after that we can't so easily put out boundless energy to pursue our passions. This is most easily seen in professional athletes, whose peak physical performance is crucial for success. But the same metabolic slowdown affects everyone, because no task is energy-free. Also by age thirty, many people who intend to get married have done so and caring for a family creates an additional energy drain.

What I have discovered is that by this phase, many people have achieved a certain degree of success based not necessarily on their inherent natural strengths but on sheer grit, self-discipline, and single-mindedness. On the surface, that appears good and is often commended. Perhaps the person has been promoted or honored with some award. But when, at age thirty, the physical body has peaked and emotional energy also begins to diminish; coupled with the energy drain caused by maintaining a marriage and raising children, it is harder and harder to stay at the front of the pack.

So a person who has been an accountant for eight or more years may begin to scratch his or her head and say, "Why has this career lost its attractiveness? Why am I more tired now? Why am I not growing?" During phase two, such people from ages thirty to thirty-five often evaluate their occupational situation and decide whether to redouble their efforts in the direction they've been going or consider a change.

This is a very important decision. Those who do not evaluate whether they are suited for their work and just put their nose to the grindstone and move ahead (or jump thoughtlessly to something else) can be in for some rough waters as they move into phase three.

Phase 3: Confirmation or Collision

I believe phase three is the most critical phase of a person's adult development. Here is the opportunity to reevaluate the adjustments made in phase two or, if no adjustments were made, to make some before there are serious health or personal consequences.

If a person made a correct decision in phase two, he or she will enjoy an accelerated rate of performance between the ages of thirty-five and forty-five. As we approach age forty-five, if we are involved in a vocation (or even avocation) that matches our inherent strengths, we begin looking forward to the reward of being a master craftsperson. It is at ages forty-five to fifty-five that we are at that zenith of our performance in our craft.

Unfortunately, those who have chosen an occupational path that does not complement their natural strengths have a sad collision awaiting them. I have witnessed hundreds of these. Not only do they face growing crises on the job, but often marital disharmony, dysfunction within the family, and medical problems will compound their occupational struggles.

Phase 4: Accelerated Performance or Devastation

Phase four usually occurs from ages forty to fifty-five. Here we find individuals riding the crest of the wave, enjoying the fruit of hard work of earlier years.

Of course, "success," however we define it, does not come automatically by finding the right job, even one well suited to our talent strengths. We also must know how to navigate life's hazardous passages if we are going to make a positive contribution in the world. Life is seldom smooth sailing. While we are honing and polishing our inherent strengths in phase two, we are also learning about life and how to get along in the world of work. We discover what it takes to put a deal together, how to read people and get along with the difficult ones, what to do about faith and life purpose, how to overcome disappointments from trusted friends, how to take risks, how to handle money, how to resolve interpersonal conflicts, the value of trust, and the importance of sincere relationships. We find out the meaning of work, what is fair compensation, and what it's like to be supervised. We then weave what we've learned into the fabric of our natural talents. If we're wiser, by age forty-five, we begin to understand what the game is all about and how to negotiate through the maze of institutions and agendas.

People who have not taken a realistic accounting of how they are gifted are at a great disadvantage even as they try to learn from their experiences in life. They may learn some basic truths about how the world turns but still not feel like they're really part of it. They are the ones who have hung on to a pension plan or guaranteed income, though it meant enduring years in an unsuitable job. They may exhibit a persistent negative attitude, hopelessness, or even passive-aggressive behavior. Their relationships deteriorate. They may be preoccupied with fear of retirement and the stress of meeting the expenses of children going to college and taking care of medical needs.

I have seen this occur even with ministers who usually are exceptionally intelligent and committed. Exhausted, they have nothing left to give their families, let alone others who are hurting. When this happens, a person has become the victim rather than the actor in his or her life, absorbing energy from other people rather than giving it to them.

Phase 5: Heightened Performance or Bitterness

The people I meet in phase five—usually between ages fifty and eighty and beyond—have either found their niche and are recognized as experts in their field, or they are depressed and bitter. Those who have found their place and who have mastered their trade enjoy a stature among their peers of relaxed confidence.

They have the energy to help others less fortunate and the optimism to survive the lumps and bumps of life. They pass down enthusiasm to their children and grandchildren. They seem to infect those around them with an unlimited supply of energy and drive even though their own bodies are physically declining. This is how most of us dream about spending our senior years. But, unfortunately, not every road leads to that future.

Why is it so difficult for people to discover who they are and what they do best?

Some would suggest that the application of common sense is sufficient for finding our occupational niche. Others would say it's all a matter of hard work and opportunity: Given a chance we can do anything if we apply ourselves. Still others—those who believe in an active God—would say it is a matter of discovering God's will for one's life. But even they are deeply influenced by what other people think God's will is. Many rabbit trails distract us from a very simple understanding of what we do best, patterns many of us were taught since childhood.

Your Six Suitcases

In an earlier book, *Unlocking Your Sixth Suitcase*, I explained the importance of cataloging our different assets when we ask, "Who am I? What can I do with my life?" I divided these attributes into six different categories, called "suitcases." By understanding what is inside each "suitcase," we begin to improve our ability to manage our life direction.

1. Work Experience or Work Skills

The first category is work experiences or work skills. In this "suitcase" are all the things that you have learned on the job, the things you do every day. This may include driving a car, programming a computer, flying an airplane, giving an injection, or teaching a class.

2. Education or Training

The second category of assets is education or training—your knowledge. These are the things that you know by reading or by being taught by someone else. Your assets in this category as well as in the first one continue to increase every day through experience and learning.

3. Personality or Temperament

In the third "suitcase" are personality and temperament, the characteristics by which others know you. These might include such qualities as graciousness, hostility, depression, warmheartedness, tolerance, nervousness, an easygoing nature, and integrity. They come, in part, from your "raw material"—your heredity—but also from the conditioning you have undergone through life, both good and bad. Sometimes these traits can be enhanced, healed, or changed somewhat if necessary by self-discipline and by a good therapist or psychologist.

4. Interests

Your interests are a great asset. They include everything from certain colors or types of food you like to certain locations that you choose to visit, the types of people you enjoy, and the hobby or leisure activities you pursue. They also include things like science, reading, the outdoors, and politics. Your interests grow and change over time—for some people, on a minute-by-minute basis, while for others they remain rather stable. But there's no guarantee that they'll remain permanent.

5. Values

Your values include what you consider right and wrong and important. Therefore, they affect attitudes concerning your family, the importance of work and what it should lead to, what you hope to accomplish in life, and the importance of relationships. Not surprisingly, your family and others close to you greatly influence your values. They also involve what you believe and therefore constitute a prominent part of your religious faith, or lack of it. Values are very deep and tend to be very important in the selection of one's life path.

In fact, before describing the sixth category, I must mention that the combination of your interests (category 4) and values (category 5) forms passion or ambition: in other words, your drive. And it is one's passion—the combination of these two categories—on which most people base their career pursuits.

A person who is interested in science and values people may go into medicine thinking the only other thing needed is academic training. Or, a person who is attracted to a lucrative lifestyle and also wants independence might choose a sales career.

A twenty-five-year-old can easily become excited—about conquering the world and joining the Peace Corps, about making the world a safer place and entering law enforcement, about needing security and joining government service. At this age, an individual has sufficient energy and drive to make up any deficiency he or she lacks in natural talent.

As I mentioned earlier, it is not until one is about thirty, moving into phase two, that a person begins to realize that things aren't coming as easily as in earlier years. Therefore, passion and ambition can be either friend or foe.

6. Natural Talents

Natural talents, the sixth "suitcase," are the attributes inherent within each person that don't change over time. They enable you to become a master craftsperson rather than a tired, broken worker who merely collects the inscribed gold watch at retirement. Talents are sometimes called aptitudes. You can discover which ones you have and learn how to use them more effectively, but you can't lose them or acquire new ones. This is a contrast to passions (a combination of interests and values), which can change over time: That is why natural talents are a better foundation for career choices.

Nevertheless, the most crucial relationship between talent strengths and occupation is that activities using our natural talents come easily while those calling on our nonstrengths come hard or not at all. We don't have to drive and strain to succeed when our natural talents are employed. That doesn't mean we shouldn't work hard at anything we do, but there is a real difference between hard work in an area of natural strength and strain in something where we have marginal talent. This is why, after age thirty, the person employing his or her natural talents seems to soar while the person struggling in nonstrength tasks runs out of gas, though by sheer grit he or she may drive on for a few more years.

I have found that every person has several natural talents—strengths sufficient to achieve several tasks exceedingly well over the course of a lifetime. Understanding and cataloging natural talents is something I've studied for over twenty years. At the office each day I help individuals evaluate their talent strengths. Appendix A lists and defines fifty-four talents. While the list is not in itself an assessment tool, examining it may suggest to you some of your talents.

Unique Purpose for Each Person

With this introduction of natural talents, we need to move to another area that has become popular in the last few years. As I have trained many professionals in the area of human resource assessment and career counseling, I have seen a renewed awareness of the spiritual dimension. Many counselors affirm the importance of spiritual empowerment to perform tasks beyond the level of natural aptitudes. I agree with the new interest in spiritual empowerment or "gifts," but these attributes are not the focus of this book.

I distinguish spiritual aptitudes as those qualities that produce supernatural results in contrast to those natural talents that are more observable, measurable, and repeatable in empowering a person to perform certain tasks exceedingly well.

The study of the supernatural took center stage for me in 1976 when I decided to leave a very secure job at the University of California in Davis as a career counselor and move to Portland, Oregon, to pursue a master's of divinity degree at Western Seminary. At the time, I had studied most all of the leading specialists in career development, yet something was missing.

Driven by a deep belief in God who, as Creator, fashioned men and women, I sought to study the Word of God, the Bible, as to what God had to say about men and women and their work. I believe that the Bible has something to say about this important area of our lives, but I found very few theological works genuinely based on the Holy Scriptures in evaluating humans and their purpose. Under the apprenticeship of some excellent professors, however, I discovered many insights, including the subject of spiritual gifts and other aptitudes.

Simply stated, I found that God not only created man and woman, but He individually endowed each one with natural talents (see Exod. 31:1–6). In Romans 12 and 1 Corinthians 12 I read about God's endowment of spiritual gifts for the performance of supernatural tasks. From these texts and others I reasoned that if the master of the universe created us with special abilities as part of His plan, then fully developing and using those capacities, if done humbly, would honor Him and give meaning and purpose to life. And, having done so, we can approach the end of our lives on earth expecting to hear, "Well done, good and faithful servant."

The Myth of the Human Superstar

My studies in human behavior and motivational training revealed a major hindrance to identifying one's life direction to achieve the status of a master craftsperson: the common presumption that we can do anything we set our minds to doing. Several years ago Napoleon Hill, a prominent motivator and business leader, coined the phrase "Whatever the mind conceives and the heart believes, I can achieve." His ideas immediately gained prominence. Institutes were set up overnight to research and champion this call to American rugged individualism called PMA—Positive Mental Attitude.

Today, this concept is the basis of many training courses, marketing schemes, franchise programs, insurance-sales programs, and almost any course titled "You Can Be What You Want to Be (all you need is a positive mental attitude, a clear focus, and plenty of determination)." Many colleges, universities, and even seminaries have adopted this theme with the promise that if you complete a degree program and remain focused and dedicated, you will succeed.

With this principle, we begin to see why children growing up in the last fifty years have become confused. They have been reared with this philosophy at school, at home, and even in church: "Whatever the mind conceives and the heart believes, you can achieve." Individuals who believe this are racking their brains to decide what they really want to do with their lives. They are told that the world is wide open, but they don't have even a hint in which direction to head. The decision appears critical because they quickly need to devote their full time, attention, and energy to its pursuit. "Do I want to travel? Do I want to work in some trade? Do I want to be a professional?" Not surprisingly, some of them freeze up and can't decide what to do.

When we understand our inherent natural talents and realize that we will go the farthest with the least amount of energy by using them, we simplify the decision-making process and achieve an inner sense of peace and confidence.

Two Types of Leadership

My study of leadership led me to some interesting conclusions. Every person—man or woman—faces the issue of leadership at some point: "Is leadership for me? Should I try for a management position?"

I believe most everyone can be a leader if he or she is willing to pay the price of hard work. The question is, What leadership ladder should one climb? I believe there are two types of leaders: leaders as supervisors and leaders as influencers. Both lead others. In fact, leaders as influencers may sometimes affect more people in more profound ways than supervisors who oversee only a portion of the lives of others.

Unfortunately, many corporations don't recognize this distinction adequately and often perceive that only those in management are leaders. People who perform well in their jobs are promoted to "leadership" positions, meaning supervising others—first a few people, then many. Tragically, too many people climb the corporate leadership ladder of supervision when they are not equipped for that role and when there may not even be any positions available at the top of the ladder. The consequences can be devastating.

The military is one organization that recognizes the foolishness of this approach. Paralleling command positions is another ladder of leadership in the form of "specialists"—including staff officers and warrant officers—who receive due respect, pay, and authority but are not required to command. They can become experts in areas other than those requiring the talents necessary for successfully supervising people.

In the stories that make up the body of this book, you will observe some problems that can occur when a person aspires to leadership and tries to lead by supervising others with much disappointment. In contrast, other characters demonstrate how people can lead others by influence when the right talent strengths are identified and used.

More Than What You Do or Know

Most likely you have an occupational stereotype of yourself, such as a police officer, bank teller, minister, second-grade teacher, professional scuba diver, or airline ticket agent. You must understand, however, that your occupational stereotype does not adequately represent who you are. You are a gifted person, not an airline ticket agent. There is nothing about being an airline ticket agent that has put an indelible stamp on you. You may have chosen to contribute your aptitudes to that occupation, and maybe it is a good fit for your talent strengths. But you can also choose to take those very same attributes and focus them in an entirely different direction.

Similarly, while knowledge is a valuable asset, your education does not define who you are. One of the best definitions for education I have found came from the late novelist, Louis L'Amour, whose books have sold over 250 million copies worldwide. He said in his work *Education of a Wandering Man*, education was "like providing a coloring book with all the dark borders drawn. We, the students, are like the children with the crayons coloring inside the lines." His definition points out that acquiring knowledge does not create something new in you but simply fills up and enhances what you already are.

In his book *Why America Doesn't Work*, Chuck Colson recalls us to the value of work when he writes, "We have forgotten the need to be a master craftsman, and we have bought the myth of security, high pay, status, and career advancement. Those are shallow life objectives, for companies are being bought out, retirement plans are being scrapped, careers are being devastated by a scribble of a pen or the stroke of a word processing key." It is a very insecure position in which to be if your whole life rests on the decision of some executive or some holding company that chooses to buy or sell the place where you work. In the stories that follow I hope to challenge you to renew within yourself the life quest of being a master craftsperson—true to yourself and to the natural strengths within you.

Five Lives . . . Five Phases

To take the principle of discovering one's talent strengths out of the theoretical realm and into the practical world, I would like to take you on a journey—a journey that follows five clients from my office files who represent a diverse range of aptitudes and lifestyles. Their stories are true, but they have been enhanced somewhat to fit the purpose of this book. Together we will walk through their life journeys, which have been divided into the five phases of adult life. We will tag along as each one navigates the passages through midlife and experience with them the impact their choices have on their job performance, marital relationships, self-esteem, and sense of personal fulfillment and life satisfaction.

But before we follow these five individuals—Diana, Jerry, Phil, Claire, and Robert—as they seek to find their own place of significance, let's meet them at the beginning of their journey: a few days before graduation at Cascade High School, 1968. If you are alert, you will begin to pick up clues to the factors that will influence their choices, goals, and future direction: their personalities, their interests, assumptions made by them and about them, their values, and yes, their natural talents and strengths. I hope you will find some of yourself in at least one of these individuals.

Our stories begin in the cafeteria on the day the Cascade Yearbook was passed out.

Chapter **1**

The Yearbook

The lunchroom at Cascade High School, always energized between fourth and fifth periods, crackled with end-of-the-year electricity. Small groups of students from the town of Waterston hunkered noisily over the tables, their food trays pushed aside. Wails of "Oh, no! I look terrible!" rose periodically from first one group, then another, interspersed with outbursts of delight, arm punching, and self-conscious laughter.

The *'68 Cascade Yearbook* had just come out.

"Diana! Diana! Over here!" yelled a group of girls gathered around a table by the windows. Diana Slater hurriedly pulled a dish of red Jell-O cubes from the dessert shelf onto her tray, paid the cashier, and threaded her way through the crowded lunchroom, clutching her yearbook against her side with her elbow.

"Your senior picture looks great, Diana!" gushed one of the girls.

"Oh, right, the Beauty Queen," Diana mocked. She was curious— she had just picked up her yearbook and hadn't had a chance to even open it yet.

"See?" said the girl, shoving her own book under Diana's nose.

A small smile twitched at the corners of Diana's mouth. She looked at the picture: Her dark hair fell over her forehead on one side and turned up into a flip, then it was tucked behind her ear on the other side. The V-necked drape all the senior girls wore for their graduation pictures set off her neck and shoulders in a nice line. Diana knew she wasn't really pretty—but she had to admit the picture had turned out well. She ought to wear her hair like that more often.

"Has Greg seen this yet?" teased one of the other girls.

"Doctor Greg you mean," someone else laughed.

Diana blushed. She wasn't used to being teased about having a boyfriend. Oh, she'd had her crushes, but most of the boys she knew were just friends, nothing more. They liked to have her on class committees and came to her for ideas about school projects or help with homework, but when it came time for weekend dates . . . the boys usually asked someone else.

Until Greg, that is. They had worked together on the Winterfest committee after Christmas, and he was interested when he found out she was active in the ski club. Diana was surprised when he had asked her out a few weeks later.

After a few more dates, people started thinking of them as a couple. It was fun having a boyfriend, but at times Diana worried about the future. Greg was interested in medicine and had received a scholarship from a prestigious university for next fall. Diana planned to attend a state college to help cut expenses. Still, it was fun to fantasize about maybe being a doctor's wife.

"Hey, Diana. Congratulations on being voted 'Most Likely to Succeed'!" said a familiar voice.

Startled, Diana looked up into the face of Jerry Cox, one of her math classmates. Jerry was only a so-so student whom she helped tutor from time to time. She knew he was a pretty good athlete—he always played football in the fall and baseball in the spring—although she rarely went to games and hadn't seen him play, but . . . there was something—she didn't know what—that made her feel kind of sorry for him.

"Thanks, Jerry," she smiled. "I haven't even seen that page in the yearbook yet!"

"Always knew you were college material," he said, giving her a thumbs up. "Go for it." Then he sauntered off to find a table with some of the other jocks.

"Ahh," winked one of the girls knowingly. "Does Greg know about your other boyfriend? A football jock, at that!"

Diana blushed again. "Don't be silly. Jerry's just a guy I know in my math class."

"Hmm, kind of cute," mused one of the other girls. "Has a neat car, too. Wish he'd ask me out."

Jerry Cox dropped into a chair at a table with some of his football teammates and bit into the apple he'd brought from home.

"Hey, Cox! Sign the team picture in the yearbook, okay?" said the baseball captain.

"Sure," Jerry said, and he scrawled his signature below the picture of himself kneeling in the front row of the team picture.

"Want me to sign yours?" asked the team captain.

"Nah . . . I mean, I didn't get a yearbook," Jerry shrugged.

"What? You didn't get a yearbook? It's your senior year, man!"

"Yeah, well . . . I just didn't want to. Probably never look at it again," Jerry said indifferently. "But what do you think about Diana Slater getting voted 'Most Likely to Succeed'?" he asked, abruptly changing the subject. He didn't want to talk anymore about not getting a yearbook, which, in spite of what he'd said, he'd really wanted. But it was one more thing that his mom, hitting the bottle as soon as she got home from work, had forgotten to pay for. He would have paid for it himself, but he didn't find out she hadn't paid his fees until it was too late; the order deadline had already passed.

"Slater?" said the star halfback, a mean running machine who could tear up a football field faster than anyone else on the team. "I would have thought it'd be that bird, Claire What's-her-name. Man, that chick has a 4.0!"

A couple of the guys snorted. "That's about all she's got. Talk about a real plain-Jane."

"Yeah, well, Slater's not a straight-A student or anything, but she's got a lot going for her. I think she deserves it," said Jerry.

"Hey, man, you got the hots for Slater?" goaded one of the guys.

"Nah. She's going with that science brain—Greg somebody—but we're kinda friends."

"Really? I didn't think she paid any attention to jocks. Too busy being on every committee the school ever thought of," said the half-back.

Jerry wished he hadn't brought it up. He didn't know if Diana would consider him a friend, but she was friendly enough in class. If he thought for a minute she wouldn't turn him down, he would ask her out . . . but the risk was too great. Being around Diana Slater always made him feel like he could be somebody instead of just an average jock. He didn't really know why. It was just that everything seemed to perk up and run more smoothly when Diana was around. On the other hand, he'd heard she was kind of religious. She'd be really turned off if she ever heard his mother's slurred speech over the phone . . .

". . . do next year?" said a voice in his ear. "Hey, wake up, Cox— I'm asking you a question! Whatcha gonna do next year?"

"Me? I dunno," Jerry shrugged again. "Probably get a full-time job. Gonna start looking right after graduation. I want to drop a four-o-nine engine into my Chevy."

"Why don't you apply for one of those athletic scholarships?" someone asked. "You've been on the team four years."

"Oh, I dunno," said Jerry, shaking his head. "I'm no star or anything."

"So? You're one of our most steady players," said the team captain.

Jerry just shook his head. He did all right on the playing field, he guessed—and he really did like to play football—but the coach never said anything to him one way or the other. High school football was one thing; college football was sure to be another. You had to be really good to get a scholarship—and he'd need a scholarship if he was going to go to college. There was no way his mom had that kind of money. His father—wherever he was—couldn't care less. As for himself, he'd put every penny he'd made into his beautiful '58 Chevy. No one had talked to him about saving for college.

"Join you guys?" asked a new voice.

Jerry looked up. "Hey, Grady. Where've you been? Sure, have a seat."

Phil Grady dumped his books on the table, took out a smashed sack lunch from his book bag, and opened a small carton of chocolate milk. "Signing the yearbook, huh?" he observed. "Sign mine while you're at it." The newcomer handed over his copy of the yearbook.

"How come you didn't turn out for baseball this year, Grady?" asked Jerry. "We could have used you. Didn't have such a hot season."

Phil grinned wryly. "At least I don't have to take the blame for it. Just kidding. Uh, I dunno. Couldn't do everything, I guess. I played trumpet in the jazz band this year . . . also signed on as designer for the yearbook, and it took a lot of time."

The other guys stared.

"You designed the yearbook? What's that mean?" demanded the football captain.

Phil looked embarrassed. "You know, decide what it's going to look like—size, type, artwork—the works. It's like a big puzzle, putting it all together."

"Didn't know you were a man of so many talents, Phil, my man!" joked Jerry.

That's what makes it so hard, Phil thought. *I never can decide what I want to do. I like sports, music, art—but I never spend enough time doing one thing to get really good.*

"Whatcha gonna do after graduation?" Jerry continued.

Phil shrugged. "Keep working at my job trimming trees for the park department."

"Haven't you been workin' for the city for a long time?" asked one of the guys. "I remember something about it back when we played junior varsity in tenth grade!"

"Yep. Summers, too, but only until Uncle Sam gets me. I signed up with the Army last week."

Several of the guys looked shocked. "You volunteered to go to Vietnam?" asked the halfback.

"Why don't you go to college? Maybe you wouldn't get drafted that way," someone suggested.

Phil shrugged. "I dunno. Figured I'd have to go sooner or later. Might as well get it over with. My grades aren't so hot—they're okay, I guess—but I don't know what I want to do. You know, choosing majors and all that."

Suddenly the guys started talking all at once about getting drafted. It hung like a hatchet over their heads as one by one they turned eighteen, but usually they didn't talk about it, as if by not recognizing the possibility, it might go away.

Phil chewed his way through the peanut-butter-and-pickle sandwich he'd made that morning ("Ugh!" his mother had said. "How can you stand that horrible combination?") and washed it down with chocolate milk as the other guys argued the pros and cons of waiting to be drafted versus signing up. He wasn't sure why he'd signed up. He didn't really know what he wanted to do. The only thing he knew for sure was that he didn't want to live at home next year, and joining the Army was a sure way to go somewhere—anywhere!

Oh, his mom and dad were all right. They worked hard at their jobs—his dad was a factory assembly worker, and his mom a secretary at the elementary school—but their lives seemed so dull, so regular. Everything at home always had to be done a certain way. There was a routine for just about everything: when to eat, where to put the tools, how to load the dishwasher. Usually he just kept his mouth shut to keep the peace . . . but inside he felt restless, like he wanted to dance wildly around the house to The Doors wailing "Come On Baby, Light My Fire," or dump all the wastebaskets into a big pile in the living room and turn all the fans on high and see what happened. Phil smiled at the thought of the grand mess that would make.

"What's so funny?" one of the guys demanded.

Phil shook his head. "Nothin' . . . Hey, did you guys check out who was voted 'Most Athletic'?"

At that there was lots of hooting as the guys thumped the football captain on the back and arms.

"Hey, you knew, didn't you?" said the captain suddenly. "I mean you designed the thing, so you knew ahead of time who was voted what. How come you didn't tell us? We're your friends—at least during baseball season!"

Phil just grinned. "Aw, you wouldn't have wanted to know. It'd be like finding your presents before Christmas."

"Yeah! Yeah!" the guys all shouted. "We wanted to know!"

"I was really voted 'Mr. Popularity'!" said the halfback, crossing his eyes and swaggering around the table.

"No, you weren't! You were voted 'Most Like Mickey Mouse'!" someone said and they started pushing each other around.

Phil snatched up his yearbook and chugged the last of his chocolate milk. These guys were his friends, but now he remembered what irritated him when he hung around them during ball season: They always talked about the same things—no imagination, no flair for the unusual.

"See ya around," he called over his shoulder as he headed for the door of the lunchroom . . . and ran straight into a girl, knocking her food tray out of her hands.

The food tray flew out of her hands and clattered to the floor before Claire Winters knew what happened.

"Hey! I'm really sorry," said the boy, bending down quickly to retrieve the tray. "Wasn't looking where I was going." He tried to salvage the food, but most of it was on the floor and he finally gave up. "Uh—I think your lunch has had it. Look, here's seventy-five cents. Better get yourself another lunch."

Claire stood rooted to the spot, feeling her face turn hot as students at nearby tables turned and stared. Some snickered. Then the boy who had run into her was digging three quarters out of his pocket.

"Oh, no . . . that's okay," she stammered, but he pressed the money into her hand and started to leave. Then suddenly, he turned back.

"Aren't you Claire Winters? The class valedictorian?"

Now Claire's face really turned hot. "Y-yes. How did you know?"

His eyebrows lifted. "I worked on the yearbook. I recognize you from your picture. A 4.0 GPA is pretty good. Congratulations. Guess we'll hear your speech at graduation. Hey, I'm really sorry about the mess."

And then he was gone.

Claire quickly found a seat at a half-empty table. She was too embarrassed to go get another lunch—at least not for a few minutes. I don't even know his name—even though he knows mine, she thought. She was pleased that he had recognized her from her yearbook picture and even noted that she had been selected valedictorian.

Wait—the yearbook! she said to herself and pulled the large volume from her shoulder bag. She quickly opened it to the page listing credits. Editor . . . copy editor . . . photographer . . . writers . . . designer. There it was: Phil Grady. She paged through the yearbook to the senior pictures in the G section . . . yes, that was him all right. She studied the picture for a few moments: dark hair worn long, friendly smile. Then she looked at the activities next to his name: freshman baseball, junior-varsity baseball, Art Club, concert band, jazz combo, marching band, yearbook.

Claire closed her eyes. What if he was interested in her? After all, he had remembered her name and said congratulations. What if he didn't have a date for the prom and asked her? For a few seconds she imagined herself in a pale blue prom dress gliding around the ballroom floor in the arms of Phil Grady . . .

Then her eyes flew open and she glanced quickly around the noisy lunchroom to see if anyone was looking at her. How stupid! Of course he wouldn't ask her. She hadn't had a date all four years of high school; what made her think she'd get asked to the prom? And even if she did, she wouldn't go. Not after what had happened with that guy at summer camp . . .

Claire shivered. It had happened last summer, when she had volunteered to work in the office of the summer camp her uncle directed. Her uncle had tried for years to get her to come as a camper, but Claire always felt too shy to live in a cabin with a bunch of strange girls, and she didn't care that much for boating and swimming and other camp activities.

But working in the office as "junior staff" was all right. She liked keeping the camp records in order and running an efficient office, and she was able to do a lot of reading in her free time. She got along well with the adult staff, who enjoyed talking to a teenager who was bright and articulate.

One of the staff members was a college guy named Ryan who helped with the groundskeeping. He often stopped by the office for one reason or another and hung around talking to her. He even sat by her at the staff dining table. Claire was so flattered that a college guy would even look at her that her heart began to pound whenever he came around. He wasn't bad looking, he seemed nice enough . . . was she falling in love?

So when Ryan asked her after supper one night if she wanted to go canoeing in the moonlight—after lights-out—she said yes. She was excited as they glided over the calm lake, sparkling with the reflection of the moon and stars, but she felt a little uneasy when he beached the canoe on the other side of the lake, away from the camp buildings. They got out of the canoe and right away Ryan began kissing her and running his hands inside her T-shirt.

"D-don't!" she tried to say.

But he just kept kissing her and saying, "You know you want to. I can tell by how you look at me." Before Claire knew what was happening, he had pushed her down and was lying almost on top of her, still kissing and touching her. With sudden strength born out of anger and fear, Claire pushed him off her and ran back to the canoe.

"Take me back to the camp right now, or I'll tell my uncle on you!" she hissed.

"Whoa," he said, smirking a little. "I'll take you back if you promise not to say anything."

So she had promised, but she probably wouldn't have told her uncle anyway. She was too embarrassed.

Now Claire shook her head as if to shake away the memory. No, she wouldn't go to the prom even if she was asked. She knew what boys wanted—especially after the prom—and she wasn't going to risk that again.

She continued to page through the senior pictures until she came to the W's. There she was, Claire Winters, looking a little lost in the black V-neck drape, her straw-colored hair hanging straight and limp around her shoulders, her thin face dominated by her unfashionable glasses. Beside her name there was only one notation: Poetry Club.

Claire sighed. *I should have worked on the school newspaper when Mrs. Jennings encouraged me to,* she thought. But at the time, she had felt too different to break into the newspaper crowd.

Her eyes fell on the picture next to her own: Robert Wilford. She knew who Robert was, all right. His smiling, confident face almost leaped off the page. He had been their sophomore class president, junior class representative to student council, and this year, student council president. He was also her closest competitor academically, but, unlike her, Robert was very popular. All the kids seemed to know and like him, and the teachers did, too. The list of his school activities was almost two inches long, and there it was: the boy voted "Most Likely to Succeed."

Well, there's one thing I've got that you don't, Mr. Wilford, Claire thought wickedly. *A 4.0, and that means valedictorian of the Class of '68. Too bad, Mr. Wonderful.*

Claire stood up. She was hungry. Why should she go without lunch just because some klutz knocked over her food tray? What did she have to be embarrassed about? Repacking the yearbook into her shoulder bag, Claire headed back for the food line with the three quarters in her hand.

Robert Wilford, the boy voted "Most Likely to Succeed," sat at a table in the center of the lunchroom holding an open yearbook and chewing on the end of his pen. He was concentrating on a blank end page with the handwritten inscription at the top, "Reserved for Rob."

He glanced up at the girl sitting patiently across the table. "I don't know, Susi. This is pretty personal. I don't want every slob reading what I'm going to write in your yearbook. After all, we've been going together six months. That's kind of hard to sum up sitting in the middle of Cascade High School's version of the Roman Arena." With a jerk of his head Robert indicated the general chaos going on around them.

Susi laughed. "Oh, all right." She took back her yearbook and stacked it on top of her other books. "I'll have my other friends sign it first, but I'm still saving that page for you." The pretty brunette sucked on the straw stuck in her milk carton, deepening the dimples in both cheeks.

"Great. I'll do it later. Promise."

Robert stretched and looked around the lunchroom. It was hard to believe that Cascade High School was almost history. He felt a pang of nostalgia. It had been a great four years. He had a lot of friends, and Susi was a terrific girlfriend: cute, good sense of humor, fun to be with. It was going to be hard to leave it all behind and start over as a college freshman next fall.

"Wish we were going to the same college next year," he said, reaching across the table and touching her hand.

"Me too." Susi sighed. "But Mom's determined that I learn French properly—in France!"

"Yeah, but that's cool. I'd like to get out of Waterston and travel sometime, too."

"You're going away to college."

"Yeah, but that's not like going to France. I want to meet different kinds of people."

"Are you still planning to major in business?"

Robert nodded. "Yeah, it makes the most sense. I'm going to be working this summer in my dad's company, and I suppose one day he's going to want me to take over the business. In fact . . . " Robert paused as he made a wry face, "if it was up to my dad, I'd forget college and just learn the ropes on the job the way he did."

"Bet your mom canned that idea!" laughed Susi.

Robert grinned. "Yeah, she's big on education."

"Well, she's right. You're really smart and you should . . ."

Susi was distracted by a thin girl with limp, straw-colored hair who marched past their table, a beaded book bag hanging from her shoulder. Susi turned back to Robert.

"Speaking of smart, there's something that bugs me. I think you should have been selected as valedictorian of our class rather than that Claire What's-her-name who just walked past. You're as smart as she is, and you sure have done more for our class. What has she ever done? Sat in a corner racking up straight-As, that's all."

Robert shrugged. "That's just it," he said mildly. "She got straight-As all four years, and I didn't. She deserves to be valedictorian."

"But . . ."

"Hey, it's not a big deal," Robert soothed. "Besides, after writing three term papers and having to prepare for the debate team finals, I'm just as glad I don't have to prepare one more speech before graduation."

Susi wouldn't quit. "But you're such a good speaker. People like what you say. I've never heard her say more than two sentences at one time. It's going to be so dull."

Robert gathered up the trash from their lunches and stacked the two food trays together. "Thanks for your loyalty, Susi, but give the kid a break. She always looks like she's expecting someone to hit her. This is her one big moment. Let her have it. It's not going to hurt us to sit through a speech. Now, come on. I want to stop by the student council office before the next period."

Robert waited while Susi gathered up her books, and then the couple pushed their way through the lunch tables toward the service window to deposit their trays.

Passionate Pursuits

A s I think back on the fresh, bright-eyed faces of people I have counseled, I have come to the conclusion that from approximately eighteen to thirty years of age, the average young adult aspires to make a difference in the world. Through twelve or more years of education, this emerging participant in the world of work has been taught that self-discipline, realistic goals, and a good education are the keys to success. So with little to guide the mind except passion and ambition, the new worker moves out to establish an identity.

In the next five chapters, as you follow each of our life travelers through phase one of his or her adult life, be alert to the factors that influence self-image, first decisions about careers, the goals they begin to pursue, and how that fits with the clues you have already picked up from "The Yearbook."

Try to pick at least one trait or experience in one of the characters that is similar to your own.

Chapter

Man on the Rise

Robert Wilford

A t college, Robert carefully selected the best fraternity and avoided those known only for their keg parties and carousing. He was more interested in maintaining his grade-point average than in getting smashed.

In his sophomore year he decided it was time to get serious about his future. What direction should he go? "The whole world is open before you," emphasized his world history prof. And Robert really felt that was true. The popularity he had enjoyed in high school seemed to mushroom in college. And the girls . . . well, they chased him. He didn't have to pursue them.

"I've been thinking about majoring in psychology," Robert told his father by phone one wintry day. There was a long silence. "You still there?"

"Oh, yeah. I was just wondering what you'd do with a psychology degree. Maybe it would be helpful. There's so much competition out there. . . . It might help in advertising. But don't you think getting a good, solid business base would be more useful? Then maybe you could take a few psychology courses on the side."

"I wasn't thinking about your company, Dad," said Robert. "I was thinking about becoming a counselor."

"How about a minister?" chimed in his mother, who was on the other extension. "They need to counsel people lots of times."

Discussions about his major always seemed to end on a tense note, so Robert decided to back off. On spring break he helped out in the family business, Wilford Electronics. Four people from the front office were out sick with the flu at the same time, so Robert manned the reception desk. It was very different from the after-hours janitorial jobs he'd had in the company as a high schooler. Everybody quickly learned who he was and treated him warmly. He liked it, and responded in his usual friendly manner.

As the school year drew to a close, he signed up for a full slate of business courses in the fall. He hadn't really given up on psychology or settled on business as his major, but keeping the door open to his dad's wishes seemed like a smart thing to do.

During his sophomore year he was active on the debate team and elected class president. He represented his fraternity on the student council and led the fund-raising effort for the local children's hospital, and he maintained a 3.2 GPA without stretching himself.

That summer he again worked in the office, filling in for a variety of people as they went on vacation. He did a little bookkeeping, made some phone sales, and planned the company picnic. Robert went to each department promoting the picnic and organizing people to plan the games, bring the food, and help with clean-up. That year more people came to the Wilford company picnic than had ever come before, and everybody loved it.

The next year at school, Robert began learning about business computers. "They're the wave of the future," he wrote his dad. "I'm certain Wilford Electronics could use one. The price tag is around $40,000, but it would put our inventory and accounting system ahead of everyone else in the field." His dad wanted time to think about it, but he promised Robert he could work on the specifics that summer . . . while he worked for Wilford Electronics.

"Dad's doing it to me again," Robert grumbled to his girlfriend. "I really wanted to travel in Europe this summer." He was getting more and more serious about Beth Carmichael, a dark-eyed girl he'd met in his Spanish class, and he didn't want to have to decide between marriage and travel after graduation. Yes, after his junior year was definitely the best time to travel. But with his dad dragging his feet, summer came and Robert ended up back at the company.

Oh, well, Robert consoled himself, *researching the computer potential was great fun.* But what he enjoyed most was visiting small companies in other fields that had computers. There he found that even though he was young, he was quickly accepted by important people. He also liked making presentations about his findings to his father and the department heads back at Wilford Electronics.

Three meetings were scheduled to consider Robert's computer proposal. At each one Robert made the preliminary presentation, although he also arranged for the computer representatives to come in and talk about the technical aspects of the plan. At the end of the third meeting, the decision was yes. As Robert walked out of the meeting, the thought struck him: I just convinced my dad and the board of directors to spend $40,000. We're going to be on the leading edge of business systems, and I did it. He felt a rush of elation and accomplishment.

During his senior year he forgot about psychology and dug into his business courses. He didn't really like them, but he did well, and they built on his experience in the company. He found it amusing that he thought of it more and more as "our" company and not just "Dad's" company. Outside of class, his debate team concentrated on state competition, and he was runner-up for the top extemporaneous speaker award.

That year Robert was also elected president of his fraternity. "So, who's surprised?" teased Beth. "You're the model of the spirit of your brotherhood. The only snag is that you graduate this year, and you're going to be a hard act to follow."

Robert laughed easily. He'd been expecting the nomination and was pleased. "If I have any problems, I'll just send any complainers to you and you can set them straight."

That was a joke, but Robert was taken off guard when a major problem did arise. He had enjoyed his popularity in the fraternity, but he had not learned that being in charge does not allow one to please all the people all the time. The fraternity rules prohibited drinking in the house: It was matter of reputation. There were other fraternities for the partiers and blow-offs; this one was for the trend-setters. But some of the guys started having Friday-night bashes in the backyard. The parties weren't all that big or rowdy, but they were against the house rules. Robert didn't know what to do. A few of the members opposed the drinking and wanted Robert to deal with the problem. This was the first time "Mr. Robert Popular" had to be the bad guy and face opposition.

"Okay, I'll speak to them," he promised.

"You'd better, because if the alumni find out about this we're going to have money problems," one of his fraternity brothers told him.

As Friday approached, Robert decided to organize a beach party among the guys who had begun drinking. That way he wouldn't have to confront them about drinking at the house. Word of the party spread and nonmembers were invited.

Then it rained and rained hard.

Before Robert could do anything about it, the party moved into the house and lasted until two in the morning. All his efforts at trying to get the guys to hold it down and cut it short only frustrated the partiers until they all seemed angry at him.

"What's the matter with you, Wilford?" asked one of the fraternity elders who was concerned about the drinking rules. "You said you were going to deal with this."

"I said I'd speak to them."

"Well, did you?"

"Look, this was planned for the beach. How was I to know it was going to pour tonight?"

"You didn't say anything about the drinking, did you?" the guy sneered. "Electing you for president was the biggest mistake I ever made."

Robert never did confront the problem and the year ended with some of the guys feeling sour and Robert realizing he was going out with less than flying colors. He made up for it by trying to appease the few who were upset with his indecisiveness. But the fraternity was soon forgotten in the flurry of his marriage to Beth. His parents' wedding gift to the new couple was a honeymoon cruise to Alaska. "Not a bad deal," Robert said, drawing Beth close as they stood at the rail of the ship watching the breathtakingly beautiful Alaskan coast slide silently by. "Getting married and getting to travel all in the same package—even if it is in the good ol' U.S.A."

Robert knew he had a job at his father's company when they returned home. He didn't know ahead of time what it would be, but he was sure that he could do something useful for the summer. On his first day on the job after the honeymoon, his father said, "I'd like you to jump into sales with both feet."

"I didn't really like the phone sales I did a couple summers ago," Robert objected.

"I don't mean phone sales; I mean real sales," his dad said.

"But that would mean clients. There's no way I could leave them in the fall if I developed a number of new accounts."

"Of course not. Why would you be leaving them in the fall?"

"Uh, well, I was thinking about going on for a master's degree . . . in business administration," Robert quickly decided. He hadn't been sure just what he'd do before then. "I'd be a lot more useful to the company down the road."

"Don't put yourself down. I never even went to college, and look at what I made of this company. We need you now, and you'd be great in sales. Actually, Robert, I'm really serious about this. We've been in a slump lately, and I think you've got what it takes to bring in some new accounts as well as increase our business with established customers. Some of them are just coasting. But if a new guy like you started working with them, they might get moving."

"I don't know, Dad," said Robert slowly. "I . . . "

"That's what I like about you, Son. You drive a hard bargain. Let me sweeten the deal. When Eddie Simpson retired last spring I didn't divide up his clients. I've been maintaining them myself . . . holding them for you. There weren't that many; Eddie had been slowing down some. But they make a solid base. It gives you a jump start. Now, is that sweet enough for you?"

The opportunity to take over established accounts was the chance of a lifetime, and Robert knew it. So, at the age of twenty-two and newly married, he became a sales representative in the family business.

Robert did well that summer. He visited all of Eddie's old clients and revived their accounts. With each contact he made a new friend and asked for additional referrals. That paid off in doubling the number of his accounts. By Christmas, Robert was number three (out of six) in total sales. But he was smart enough to pass on to other reps the names of potential customers who were located in their territory. At first some of the other salesmen dropped the ball, and Robert wondered whether he'd done the right thing. But all five appreciated the contacts he had passed their way, and before long his enthusiasm did just what his father predicted; it inspired the other reps to work harder, and they didn't seem to resent his success.

The result for the company was an unprecedented 11 percent growth in overall sales in the third quarter. And the fourth quarter got off to such a good start that Robert's father declared a Christmas bonus equal to one week's pay for all seventy employees. Bonuses had been rare at Wilford Electronics. Usually there was nothing more than the traditional Christmas turkey. But even when there had been more, no one could remember anything larger than a twenty-five-dollar check.

"It's Robert, the old man's son," began the rumor. "He's pumping new life back into the company."

Do you remember the last time someone shook your hand and in that first few minutes you felt you had known him or her all your life? Robert has that experience with everyone he meets. It's not something he consciously does or even notices. It comes naturally, and he thinks it happens to almost everyone else.

This enviable ability had paid off handsomely in high school, where he was the center of attention in sports as well as student government and easily won the favor of most of his teachers. He also could think on his feet and communicate easily in front of others as a speaker.

Up to this point in his life, Robert has never faced an obstacle that he didn't feel he could overcome with a little effort. His biggest challenges have been sporting events, competition on the debate team, and student-body elections. He never felt the embarrassment or agony of trying to attract girls, since they were usually standing in line to go out with him. When he applied for some position or pursued some goal, people usually thanked him for doing so. He did not have to endure the repeated rejections most people face before achieving success.

You and I have probably known many Roberts. But before you decide this is the dream you would like to live out (or wish your children could live), you should know that Robert is in for some surprises. There are some challenges in store for him of the kind we seldom hear about. Let's wait and see what happens as Robert moves into phase two.

Chapter

Campus Organizer

Diana Slater

O n her way out of the house, Diana checked the mailbox one last time. She was off to college.

The mail had come, but there was no letter from Greg. He hadn't written for three weeks. Somewhere deep inside, Diana knew what that meant. She had hoped all summer that Greg's reason for staying back in Chicago was as he had said: "Just for the job. Premed at Northwestern is expensive, you know." But he could have found a job back home in Waterston for the summer if he had wanted to be near her. Besides, the letters had slowed until . . .

Maybe it's all for the best that we can't afford Northwestern, Diana thought as she marched out to the car with her last suitcase. *Mid-Valley State is probably just as good as Northwestern anyway, even though it's not a Ivy League school.* She threw her luggage in the trunk, slammed the lid, and climbed in the backseat. *Besides, I wouldn't want to seem like I was chasing Greg.*

"You okay, Honey?" her mom asked.

"Yeah. Let's just get going."

"You'll be just fine once you get settled. You always land on your feet." Her dad backed the car out of the driveway and cruised down the street.

And, as her father had predicted, Diana did just fine without Greg. She joined a "sensible" sorority and got right to work maintaining her solid B average. To help with expenses, she found a job on campus working about twelve hours a week. But college life seemed rather tedious to Diana. She didn't really know why she was there. She never heard from Greg again, but hometown friends would pass along gossip about him from time to time.

Most of the guys at college seemed to look right past Diana, so she only rarely was asked out on first dates, and never second ones. "You scare them off," said her roommate.

"Come on," Diana protested. "I may not be a beauty queen, but I'm not that bad looking. There are a lot of girls more homely than I who get dates every week."

"No, no. It's not how you look. It's just that . . . that you take charge too much. Guys don't like to be dominated."

Diana didn't ask what her roommate meant. She wasn't sure she really wanted to know. *If I "dominate" them,* she thought to herself later, *then they must be Milquetoasts.* She decided to concentrate on her studies. If "Mr. Right" was around, he'd find her soon enough.

But the next fall changed Diana's experience of college. She was attracted to a small discussion group that met weekly to discuss the Bible. Never before had she known religious students who were so intellectual. They wrestled with the implications of what Francis Schaeffer called "the post-Christian world" and read things like Schaeffer's *The God Who Was There* and C. S. Lewis's essay, "The Problem of Pain." Then Diana met Jim Barber, one of the student leaders. Suddenly college was more than she'd ever hoped for. "These people are exciting," she wrote home to her folks. "I don't understand half of what they are talking about, but they are genuine, with no put-ons, and they are trying to make a difference in the world. It's all so neat."

Jim was a junior, planning to go on to seminary. But while he was at Mid-Valley State, he had ideas for starting a coffeehouse ministry. "I've been to several coffeehouses," he told Diana one day. "People—usually students—come all the time and sit around and talk. Sometimes there's live folk music. I think our campus club should start one. It'd be great for outreach."

The next day as Diana walked to work, she noticed a vacant storefront for rent near the campus. She called the number on the sign and found out that the owner would be glad to rent it to a student group for $150 a month. She called the pastor of the church Jim attended that she had visited. She asked him if he thought there were any businessmen in town who would support a coffeehouse outreach to the campus. He didn't know but referred her to the local church businessmen's association. After four more calls, Diana had tentative pledges to cover the monthly rent, plus some one-time seed money to open. "After that," the businessman said, "I think it ought to be able to carry its own in terms of coffee and utilities, don't you?"

Diana agreed and couldn't wait to tell Jim her good news. She couldn't find him that night but talked to three other students who volunteered to staff the coffeehouse.

The next day when she found Jim, she met him with: "I think we ought to call it the Colloquy; don't you?"

"The what? What are you talking about?"

Diana laughed as she realized how far she'd taken Jim's idea without ever checking in. "I didn't mean to jump out ahead of you or anything," she apologized as she filled him in. "But if you don't think it is a good idea, we can always change it."

"Oh, no. It's fine. I just could never have pulled it off . . . at least not this fast." He stared at her in amazement, really seeing her for the first time. Diana blushed.

Diana planned the decor, scheduled the program, and coordinated the volunteer staff. Jim explained the idea of a coffeehouse to the student leaders and made three brilliant presentations to local churches asking for their prayer and financial support.

The Colloquy opened Halloween night.

This was the beginning of their dating relationship. Diana was proud of how Jim could sit down with people over a cup of coffee and get them to open up about deep personal things. Somehow he just knew how to pick up on where they were hurting. He was also great at giving short talks—on almost any subject, it seemed to Diana—that had a spiritual component. It wasn't "preaching"; it just raised the right questions. It was something she could never do.

But she sure could organize a good coffeehouse. And as the year progressed, so did their relationship.

Jim graduated the next spring. He applied to and was accepted by Faith Evangelical Seminary, about four hours north of Mid-Valley State. "It's not so far away," he reassured Diana. "We'll be able to get together from time to time." But Diana remembered what had happened to Greg when he had gone to Northwestern.

During the next year Jim was faithful enough. He wrote regularly and made every effort to get together with her on holidays and even during three-day weekends. On Christmas break he spent two days at her family's home, and she spent a weekend with his family. They weren't officially engaged, but things were getting serious. Their joy was tempered only by the pain of separation.

Over spring break he said, "You know, Diana, you could transfer up to Faith College for your senior year. It's connected with the seminary, and they do have a strong program in early-childhood development. You might have to pick up a couple extra Bible courses or something, but you could do it, and we could be together."

"I don't know," said Diana, fighting with the deep longing inside her. "At this point it might just be harder to be seeing each other all the time."

"Well, if that's the problem," he grinned, "then we'd better get married. Would you? I mean, would you marry me?" And he dropped down on one knee.

"Are you serious?"

"Of course! You know how much I love you."

They were married Sunday afternoon, June 6, 1971, found an apartment not far from the seminary, and Diana Slater Barber finished her bachelor's degree the next year at Faith College.

The reality of preparing to be a pastor's wife to Jim was far more exciting than her high school dreams of being a doctor's wife to

Greg. She became active in the seminary wives' club and, realizing that she should do something to socialize, thought she would like to be the next president.

She wanted the position because she saw so much that could be done for the wives. First, there was no coordinated plan for child care. The seminary families hired some of the college students as baby-sitters, but there was no established rate, which often created problems. Also, there were many times when, with just a little coordination, the wives could have covered for each other rather than hire someone. Second, Diana wanted to organize shopping-trip pools so that the wives could save on travel to the grocery stores and provide company for each other. And finally, she wanted to start a women's Bible-study group. The seminary classes for wives were fine, but they were different from the kind of support that could come from studying the Bible together. She mentioned her ideas to a few of the other wives and dropped a hint that she wouldn't mind working for those things. "We'll nominate you for president, then," they said.

But before the election, the outgoing president took Diana aside and said, "You can't do this Bible-study thing. It will just stir up hard feelings with the administration."

"What do you mean?" asked Diana.

"You don't see any women professors on campus, do you?"

"No, except for Martha Wilson, who teaches a class on children's ministry part-time."

"That's because women aren't supposed to teach the Bible. Even the classes open to wives are taught by men."

"But I'm not going to teach a seminary class or preach or even pastor anyone. It's just a Bible study."

"Well, be forewarned. I'm not in favor of the idea. We've worked too hard to be called in by the dean."

Diana was floored. How could anybody who was preparing for the ministry behave in that fashion? But she did not tell Jim about the incident.

At the next wives' club meeting, one of her friends nominated her and said, "Diana has some good ideas for our club that I think we ought to hear before the election." So Diana stood up and briefly mentioned baby-sitting and carpooling but spent most of her time explaining the Bible-study idea. She was not going to be intimidated.

However, true to her warning, the outgoing president stood up and said, "Let's not forget that our seminary has not encouraged women to teach the Bible. I would recommend choosing a president who has been married a little longer, someone whose greater experience can be a good example to the younger wives." She dragged "younger" out. Then she nominated another woman.

The other nominee won.

The experience was so devastating to Diana that she could not bring herself to attend the next, and year-end, meeting. She didn't want to be a bad sport, but knowing the former president was still in charge was frustrating. So she concentrated on her studies and graduated with honors with a major in early childhood development.

Are you puzzled by Diana's biography at this point, or does she fit a stereotype you have observed? I recall the Dianas I knew in high school and college. As a somewhat insecure male in those days, I avoided them at all costs. It wasn't anything in particular that they did; they just took charge so much that I felt even more insecure. Now, many years later, when I meet someone like Diana, I gladly help her take full charge of all the horsepower that she commands.

As a little girl, Diana was probably the one who always organized the neighborhood activities and dominated them. Do you remember a girl like that, who could bat better than most boys and took charge during youth group activities and at church was the youth minister's right-hand helper? If Diana had not come from a supportive environment it would have been easy for her to develop an inferiority complex or become angry because she was not like other girls. Her drive to take charge comes from her innate ability to assume command. When Diana was growing up in the fifties and sixties, this was not an acceptable role for women. She could easily have become angry and caustic. But fortunately for Diana, she came from a stable home that affirmed her and made her feel normal even when she didn't receive that affirmation from her peers.

Today there are more accepted leadership roles for women both in religious circles and in the world of work.

As we view Diana in this chapter, we see that she has experienced a lack of understanding from other women. Yet we see the obvious capacity she has for making things happen and the corresponding confidence other people have in her. We notice a curious blend of aptitudes between herself and Jim, which will be interesting to follow throughout the rest of her life. Neither of these individuals completely understands the depth of how they are talented. They work very well together as a team, and their success will suggest that their marriage was made in heaven. As we move into the next chapter of Diana's life, look for the way she begins to understand who she is and how that influences her identity, her marriage, and her outlook on life.

Chapter 4

Landing That Good Job

Phil Grady

Y ou will be out in the company street, dressed, in formation, and standing at attention at o-four-hundred. Is that understood?" barked the drill sergeant as he paced the aisle between the bunks.

Once he had passed by Phil, Phil's hand instinctively went up to feel the strange stubble on his head. It itched.

Without turning around the sergeant yelled, "What's the matter with you, Mr. Grady? Don't you know what 'attention' means?"

Phil's hand dropped to his side as his back stiffened. He and the other recruits, dressed only in their underwear, were standing at the feet of their bunks. "No, Sir. . . . I mean, yes, Sir."

"'Sir?'" roared the sergeant as he wheeled around and came back to stand so close to Phil that only the flat brim of the sergeant's Smoky Bear hat separated them. "Do you see any bars on my shoulder?"

"No."

"'No,' what?"

"No, Sir," managed Phil.

"'No, Sergeant!'" corrected the drill instructor, his face so red that Phil thought it would burst.

"No, Sergeant," complied Phil.

"I can't hear you. You better sound off if you ever hope to become a soldier in this man's army!" Tiny droplets sprayed Phil as the sergeant bellowed in his face.

"Yes, Sergeant!" Phil yelled.

"Well, make up your mind." The sergeant turned and stalked to the end of the barracks before he turned back to face the recruits. "Are there any other questions?" He waited. "I said, 'Are there any other questions?'"

"No, Sergeant!" chorused the men as they finally picked up their cue.

"O-four-hundred, gentlemen," he said, and the lights snapped out.

Phil fumbled in the dark. The recruits had just boxed up their civilian clothes and other personal possessions and sent them home. There was a bag of Army-issue things in his footlocker and folded blankets on the bed. He spread the blankets clumsily and crawled in. *How did that sergeant know my name?* he wondered. *How did he see me scratch my head when his back was turned?* It dawned on Phil that perhaps joining the army might prove to be a painful mistake.

But he made it through basic training. Actually, his high school job with the park district as an assistant tree trimmer had trained him so he had a lot of confidence when it came to physical conditioning and running obstacle courses. He went on to cooks' school for his advanced individual training. After that, he was sent to Vietnam with the 101st Airborne. There he was assigned to the battalion kitchen, preparing hot meals for the enlisted mess. He often rode the chopper out to a firebase to serve the men on field maneuvers.

"Hey, Grady, you going back to HQ right away?" asked a short spec four with a downy mustache. His name tag read "Bettencort."

"As soon as we break down the line and mount up," Phil said as he spooned the extra gravy and potatoes out onto the ground, a practice that was against regulations, not because of waste, but so the enemy wouldn't eat it that night.

"Mind taking something back for me?"

"No problem. What is it?"

The soldier pulled a fat packet from inside his sweat-stained T-shirt. "Acapulco Gold," he said as he glanced around and then handed it to Phil.

"Where'd you get that? Isn't the local stuff good enough for you?"

"More mellow. Just keep it for me. When I rotate in, we'll party. It'll blow your mind."

"Heavy," said Phil, as he tossed the packet into an empty thermos.

Two days later when Phil rode the same circuit, he didn't see the young specialist in the chow line. "Where's Bettencort?" he asked a tall sergeant with a once-red sweatband around his head.

"Bought the farm . . . last night."

"How?"

"'Sniper fire,' the report says."

"What?"

"He was setting out Claymores when one went off. Guess those gook snipers are gettin' downright cunning. Look," the black sergeant said, leaning close. "Bettencort was stoned. Who knows what happened?" Then he moved on through the line.

Phil kept serving gray peas with one scoop and runny mashed potatoes with the other as one or two guys at a time came in from the perimeter to get their food.

That night Phil opened the packet and rolled three joints. He went out by himself and smoked one right after the other until he couldn't even crawl. "Years" later it began raining—sometimes marshmallows, sometimes bullets. Through it all he had only one sane thought: *I must keep my face out of the mud, or I'll drown.*

He managed just that until he was rotated back to the states to finish up his hitch at Fort Benning, Georgia. He did not re-up for a second tour in Nam.

"I'm not even going to ask you," said his company first sergeant. "They wouldn't want you over there again. You're always messing with the food. You put cinnamon in the coffee and peanut butter on the brownies. You want to paint the mess hall peach. You can't leave good enough alone. You're not army."

A year and a half later when he was discharged, Phil returned to Waterston and moved in with his parents. They were glad to have him home safe from the war, but his old room felt like a cell. It wasn't that it was dark and dingy; there was a nice window overlooking the park. But Phil felt as if he was in a time warp. He didn't belong there. Everything was so rigid. "A place for everything, and everything in its place," his father had always said, and he still lived that way. It was worse than the army. At least in Nam nobody cared.

"I think I could get you in at the plant," his dad said one day. "I was talking to the union steward, and he said they are going to need some more guys on the line."

"I don't think I'm ready for the plant," Phil said.

"Well, sure. You deserve a vacation. A guy serves his country and he's earned a break. But you've been back three weeks now, and I wouldn't want this opportunity to pass you by."

"Thanks, Dad. I'll think about it."

Two weeks later his dad said, "They put two new guys on the line today."

"I've been thinking about trying something else, Dad. I don't think I would fit in at the plant."

"Well, it's been pretty good to me. Of course, being the machinist and all, it's a little better than assembly. But if you got on, I could maybe pull some strings to get you a better position. Jobs aren't so easy to find these days, you know."

"I know, Dad. I might go check out tree trimming again."

"Ah, Son. There's no future in that. That isn't even a civil-service job. Even your friend, that Mexican kid, what was his name? He was just a couple years older than you."

"Ramirez?"

"Yeah, Ramirez. Anyway, he quit."

"Oh, yeah? What's he doing now?"

"Joined the fire department, I heard."

The next day Phil went to the local fire station and asked for Ramirez. Maybe he could get on at the fire department.

"I think he's over at Station D," said a fireman sweeping an already spotless floor.

Phil felt kind of funny as he drove across town to Station D. Maybe the feelings came with fitting back into civilian life. He'd been warned to expect a lot of adjustments. But somehow he doubted he was doing the right thing. But I've got to get a job, he thought. And certainly being a fireman ought to have its benefits: job security; one day on, two off; a little excitement now and then; decent pay.

He found his old friend watching an afternoon game show on TV. "We're not supposed to watch TV during the day," said Ramirez like a kid caught with his hand in the cookie jar. "But the old man doesn't mind if everything is shipshape, so who cares. But hey, man, look at you. I heard you were back. How you doin'?"

Phil said he was okay and slowly guided the conversation around to asking about getting a job at the fire department.

"Well, yeah. They're always having qualification tests. One's coming up in a couple weeks, I think. But don't worry, man. If you qualify and can cook, we'll take you. Who cares if you can fight fires or not? The food these guys fix can kill you."

Phil went to the city hall and picked up an application. It came in a large, thick envelope that he thought must contain brochures or information sheets, but it was just an application . . . sixteen pages long.

A week after turning in the application, he was called in for tests. They lasted all day. The morning involved the physical fitness and agility tests, not too hard after his military training. In the afternoon Phil took a long written exam of his mechanical aptitude and general common sense, it seemed to him.

A week later he was called in to take a lie-detector test—of all things—and receive a psychological exam and an IQ test. Then there were two personal interviews. At each step, Phil could have quit. But it had become a challenge to him, and he wasn't about to give up. The day he was finally sworn in was like a real triumph.

He started the firefighter's academy the next Monday morning. "I'm really proud of you," his mother said as he finished his coffee and headed out the door. "Do you know when you'll be home this evening?"

"Not 'til I get here, Mom."

The training was exciting. Mornings were spent in the classroom, and the afternoons involved practical work with the hoses and air packs, and running obstacle courses. They even did a live burn of an old house that was slated for demolition in order to get experience.

But eight weeks later, after he had proudly graduated, Phil discovered another side of being a fireman. As the newest rookie, he was given all the drudgery jobs. He was the first one expected to begin a job and the one who had to remain to the bitter end when finishing it. The other men picked on him and made him the butt of all the jokes. All this didn't bother him. He was a good sport and could take it as well as he could dish it out. He knew that someday there'd be someone newer than he, and he could move up in the pecking order.

But what bothered him was how picky everyone seemed to be about having everything in order. Each morning he had to set out each man's cup of coffee. But they had to be in order and each filled exactly to the brim, and the moment anyone's spilled, he was called to clean up the mess. "There's a place for everything, and everything should be in its place," the lieutenant told him the first day. And that just grated on him.

But so what? He was a fireman, and he had never felt prouder than when he was coming back from their first real fire call. A fire in someone's basement had started in a pile of rubbish. The basement was so full of smoke that it was impossible to see, but everyone did just as Phil had learned in training. He didn't make any mistakes, either. They found the fire and put it out quickly with no structural damage. Hey, he was a fireman!

Many of us emerge from adolescence as Phil did: nothing unusual, everything normal, good family, normal grades, acceptable performance, good friends—in other words, mediocre. But Phil—as all of us are—is gifted with capacities that can lead to excellence. Phil illustrates a common profile found in many of my clients. At this point, he is back from the army and beginning his first job. But without his realizing it, a curious conflict has been developing.

Phil comes from a home where things were always kept in their place. His room was cleaned up daily. Dinner was served on time.

The garden rake and shovel always were hung in the same place. Even the soiled rags were washed, neatly folded, and put away. As a youngster, when Phil wanted to experiment and try different things, his parents corrected him and instructed him on how things ought to be done.

Early on Phil began realizing that the "correct" way of doing things didn't always fit the way he wanted to do them. He did not intend to rebel; he just saw things differently. But he learned that there wasn't any use in asking why or fighting his parents' way.

If you respond by saying, "So what's wrong with being orderly?" don't worry. There's not necessarily anything wrong with it, but your response does tell something about your organizational talent strengths. On the other hand, if you are like Phil, you grew up with an intense desire to challenge everything just because there might be a better or different way to do it. You always had a new idea, maybe two or three. Maybe you felt quite restricted when you did not have freedom to try doing things a new way. Maybe your tendency to do things differently was labeled "rebellion" even though you didn't intend to be rebellious.

Phil's parents were supportive, loving, and affirming; but both Mom and Dad placed a very high priority on "a place for everything, and everything in its place." This went against Phil's urge to experiment. Isn't it interesting that some of us are gifted with a creative bent that seeks to constantly question, probe, and evaluate? We find it very uncomfortable to have to live with extreme orderliness.

All Phil knew was that he felt confused and out of place, and he assumed most of his friends felt that way, too. Yet because of his strongly structured upbringing, he developed some admirable habits of orderliness that allowed him to survive in the military and even qualified him for his first job. But as Phil grows older, this internal conflict of exploring new ideas versus maintaining established order will surface and begin to cause a very typical life and career burnout. This conflict will impact his self-image, his reevaluation of his childhood, his marriage, and his ability to work for an employer.

Chapter 5

The Paper Chase

Claire Winters

D on't worry, Honey, you'll love Carlisle. It really should be considered an Ivy League school. When your father and I went there, half the faculty were from Cambridge or Oxford. It has a very old-world feel."

"But I won't know anybody," Claire said as she peaked the meringue before sliding the pie into the oven.

"So what? You'll make new friends. College friends are the best, anyway. It's only when you are in a university setting that you are truly able to meet your peers, people of your caliber. It won't be like most of these kids you have known in high school."

"I know, Mom, but it's only three weeks away. Maybe I should have traveled for a year."

"You wouldn't have known anybody in Europe."

"I know, but . . ."

Three weeks later Claire was alone in her dorm room arranging her things on her dresser. She had no idea what her roommate would be like and wished her parents would have stayed at least through the afternoon when everyone was supposed to arrive on campus. *But what difference does it make?* she chided herself. *It's not like I could walk out and go home at this point. I'll just have to make do.*

But Claire's roommate was no problem: Lisa came from a wealthy family in Brazil, was quiet, and kept mostly to herself. She and Claire had one thing in common: They liked to keep their things orderly. They got along so well that they planned to room together all four years. But Lisa didn't return for her senior year: Claire got just one brief letter explaining a pregnancy and a quick marriage.

Her new roommate nearly drove Claire crazy. Not only did she never put her own things away but she also borrowed Claire's hand mirror, socks, and other belongings without putting them back. Even when she borrowed Claire's typewriter, she would move the tabs and not reset them, or go off and leave the machine running. "If you insist on using my stuff, why can't you put things back the way you found them?" Claire screamed one day.

"Hey, calm down," the girl said. And then she turned to the three friends she had invited into their room without asking Claire and said, "Forgive my roomie. She's got a very heavy hang-up with materialism."

How Claire survived that year she never knew. Maybe it was the internship she got working at the *Globe*, the local newspaper. There she felt appreciated. She was given a desk—with which no one messed. She did a lot of typing, but she also maintained research files for one of the editors and frequently did proofreading for him. He wasn't threatened when she caught errors. "Better to catch them before rather than after publication," he always said.

The *Globe* was far removed from the Elizabethan literature that had become her major. But it did get her close to printed word, and that gave her the opportunity to fancy herself a writer even though she was never asked to do even the obituaries. She decided she wanted to stay with the paper even after graduation.

"But, Mom, you don't understand. I know I don't have to work. I appreciate that you and Dad plan to pay for grad school. But I like this job. I want to get an apartment and support myself for the summer. Then I can continue on part-time next fall."

"How can you go to grad school if you are trying to work? You'll spread yourself too thin," said her mother. "There must be some young man up there who has bewitched you."

"No, Mom. I just want to spend the summer on my own. I like the job. The newspaper's interesting."

"Well, what do you do?"

"I'm an assistant to one of the editors. I do some editing myself. It's all connected to my interest in literature."

"I've never considered journalism very close to literature. But if that's what you want, your father and I are happy for you. You will come and see us for a vacation, won't you?"

"Of course, Mom. I was planning on taking off the first couple weeks in August. Okay?"

Claire found an apartment. She had no furnishings, just her books, stereo, and other things from college. She didn't want her parents to pay for everything, so she scrounged. She built a bookcase from bricks and boards. She got a mattress and put it on the floor. (It made her feel kind of Bohemian.) She found an old rocker, a table and two chairs, and various unmatched kitchen utensils from a secondhand shop. The apartment became functional and neat, if not cozy or inviting. But that didn't matter: Claire didn't have to impress many guests. It was home, it was hers, and nobody messed with her things.

Her mother's predictions about developing "best friends" in college hadn't proved true. Lisa had been a good roommate but not a close friend, and Claire just never seemed to get to know anyone else that well. But grad school proved different. Classes were small—six to eight people—and their interest in literature was so specialized that she was often with the same people in several classes. She became best friends with Esther. Like Claire, Esther was somewhat reserved. Then Esther introduced Claire to David Sorenson, a married accounting student. Actually, he was a couple years older than Claire and was taking the one course he needed to graduate. He already had a good job with a local firm and was like Claire in many ways—quiet, neat, and interested in detail. As a friend, Claire considered him "safe" because he was married. What Claire did not know was that David's marriage was in trouble.

Someone who didn't know this trio might have thought them hippies, with their long stringy hair, black clothes, and David's beard, but that was not the case.

They kept journals, which they often read to each other, and critiqued plays. Claire wondered why David had become an accountant; he loved to talk about the most esoteric details when discussing literature.

It was through hearing David read from his journal that Claire discovered his marital tension. She found it hard to respond to his pain and frustration verbally, so she wrote him letters in which she expressed her sympathy and understanding. He always thanked her for them.

Claire continued working at the *Globe*. She let her parents pay her tuition and rent but prided herself in covering her other expenses. It gave her a cherished feeling of independence. Still, on her income she knew it would be hard to fully support herself even if she were working full-time. Though her skills as a researcher and proofreader had become valuable, she was technically classified as a midlevel secretary. The one time Claire asked about it, her boss replied, "You're a unique case, Claire. None of our current job descriptions fit you. You don't actually work in the proof room, so we can't call you a proofreader. You research only part of the time, so we can't classify you as a researcher. But you do work with me, keeping me organized, so 'secretary' is the best we can do. But don't get me wrong. You're far more valuable to us than a mere secretary."

What he didn't tell her was that he could have easily classified her as an assistant editor, and that would have fully described what she did. But it would have also meant a substantial increase in pay. Claire did not ask about her classification again. Her job was secure, and she was doing things she liked, and that seemed better than rocking the boat.

As the time approached for her to receive her doctorate, Claire began to panic. What was she going to do? "You think you're scared?" asked Esther. "You've got a job you like. You can stay there until something better comes along. But me, I've got to hustle. I've got tuition bills to pay, and I still haven't found a good teaching position."

Teaching was the last thing Claire wanted to do, and since she hadn't gotten very far with her writing career, it seemed like a good idea to stay put. She could go full-time with the newspaper and still write in the evenings. Nonetheless, she dreaded Esther's leaving. A friend as good as Esther was hard to find.

Claire was seeing less and less of David. She attributed it to her busyness in completing her dissertation and his getting established in his accounting firm. Then one day he stopped by to say that his wife had left and filed for divorce. "I'm not going to fight it, so it'll probably go through rather quickly. We already worked out how to divide up the property. Am I glad we don't have any kids. Somehow I just knew it wasn't time."

"David, what's happened? I didn't know it was that bad. Why aren't you going to fight it?"

"No sense in fighting it. That would prolong the misery. In the end, she'd be granted the divorce anyway."

"But maybe in the meantime something would happen to bring her to her senses. Maybe you could get some counseling or something and get back together."

"Maybe . . . but I'm not sure I'd even want that. I actually don't know why I ever married her; we have so little in common. She's nothing like you." David stopped abruptly as he realized what he had said.

Claire stared at him, then turned away. "They're . . . they're moving our offices," she stammered.

"What?"

"I said the newspaper is moving to a new building."

"Oh. Well, that's nice."

"Not really. It's going to mess up everything."

"What do you mean?"

"I mean, it'll take months before things get settled again. I was supposed to take vacation the week of the move."

"Sounds like a great plan: Let them do the whole thing," said David.

"And move my desk?" said Claire with horror.

"Sure. You weren't thinking of strapping it on your back and packing it down the street, were you?"

"No. But I've got to be there, or they'll never get everything arranged properly. I don't even know what office I'll be in or anything. Maybe I don't even belong at the *Globe*. My mom says it's a waste job, that they didn't pay for a golden Ph.D. just so I could be a glorified secretary."

"You'll make it," assured David. "But maybe you should be doing something else. Who knows?"

David stopped by more often after that. The divorce went through in three months, and Claire adjusted to the newspaper's move. "I guess it's not so bad," she told David over dinner one night. "I've got my own office—well, not a real office, but a carrel with head-high dividers."

"What did you have before?" asked David.

"Just a desk in a room with about six other people."

"Did they give you a promotion to go with it?"

"As a matter of fact, they did. I'm now an editorial assistant."

"That's no promotion. That's just what they call secretaries in the publishing industry these days."

"No it's not. The *Globe* has secretaries, too. And I'm not one of them."

"Claire, they're taking advantage of you. You've got your Ph.D., after all."

"But it's in Elizabethan literature. How does that benefit a local newspaper?"

"Then get a job somewhere else . . . where you can use that degree."

"You sound like my parents."

When her parents had said the same thing all those times, she had brushed it off as meddling. But David's saying it started Claire thinking. She did not, however, like the feelings that came with the idea. Where could she get another job? What was she suited to do? She still hadn't had more than a few small articles published, so her dream of becoming a writer was fading fast. But teaching seemed like the only other option. She was caught like so many other students—with no place to go.

Before she had found the answers to these questions, however, David suggested something that put them out of her mind. "Why don't we get married?" he asked one night on their way home from a play. The shock left Claire speechless. They had been seeing each other almost every day, and she couldn't deny that she had fantasized about marrying him, but he had never even tried to kiss her. What was up? Did he love her, or was this just a proposal of convenience?

"Well, I don't know. Why?"

"'Why?' Because I love you." And then he did kiss her like she had never imagined a kiss could be. Her revulsion of Ryan, the guy who had tried to force himself on her at summer camp, flashed through her mind. It was a high school memory she'd thought she had forgotten. She considered it only a moment; this was different. She pushed the memory away and kissed David back. They were married the following March, three weeks before Claire's twenty-eighth birthday.

Claire Winters introduces us to the hidden, quiet world that often represents the depth and quality of the people in business, technical fields, and educational institutions. We may feel a sense of pity as we read about her because we remember watching and perhaps laughing at kids in high school and earlier years who were not in the mainstream, who appeared awkward and definitely were not part of the "in" group.

Yet, as we are beginning to see, Claire—a very gifted person with academic intellect, a sense of order, and a flair for writing—has formed a foundation upon which she will build over the years and begin to contribute richly to society. Claire is like many people who make noteworthy professors, scientists, doctors, accountants, lawyers, novelists, archaeologists: gifted to perform tasks and complete projects that require long, tedious hours of study and evaluation. With focused attention they impact the lives of many people, whether in medicine, research, psychology, literature, or other fields. It's the Claire Winterses that write our textbooks and that magazines and newspapers quote as experts, yet who receive little recognition. Here we can observe firsthand exactly how this life unfolds, much like a mystery, to some noteworthy achievement.

At this point, Claire is still confused, wondering what is wrong with her, but she is beginning to hold tenaciously onto something important: the work she has done. She has learned to attribute value to her work beyond what society places on it. She has not yet learned how to position herself to show the productivity and the contribution that she can make, but it is to be hoped that, as the years unfold, that will take place.

It is fortunate that she has a strong foundation of loving affirmation. Most likely her parents live quiet lives. Her father is a senior scientist for a research institute; both he and her mother are well educated. Now this new relationship with David appears to provide a support system that will give her the confidence to step out boldly and overcome the social inhibitions that held her back in her earlier years. We might see Claire as a rosebud just beginning to open to display her full beauty.

Chapter 6

NFL Superstar

Jerry Cox

Jerry rolled up the window of his customized '58 Chevy. The fall air had a nip to it. *Where are those guys?* he wondered as he strained to see into the brightly lit grocery store. But there were so many signs in the windows that he couldn't see much of anything inside.

Then the door flew open and Roger and Jack came running out. Roger tumbled into the backseat. Jack handed a bag to Roger and then piled into the front seat. "Step on it," he commanded as he slugged the dashboard.

"Yeah, man," said Roger. "Move it!"

"What did you guys get?" asked Jerry, his big four-o-nine rumbling to life. He backed up slowly.

"Come on, Jerry. Let's get out of here," Jack pleaded.

"Take it easy," Jerry said as he eased the raked, canary yellow Impala over the potholes and onto the country road. "I don't want to leave my pipes back there in the parking lot."

"Go, man, go! I bet this thing can't do a hundred in a quarter."

Jerry bit on the challenge and punched the throttle to the floor. The four-o-nine roared like a jet, the big slicks smoking and screaming as the Chevy fishtailed down the road.

Dazed, and with blood trickling down his forehead, the store clerk pulled himself to his feet and peered out the window. Six bullet taillights disappeared into the night.

"Look, Son. You need to know that I am going to have a very hard time defending you under the circumstances."

"But I didn't rob that store," protested Jerry as he paced around the small room in the police station. He'd already spent three nights behind bars and didn't see why the arraignment that afternoon wouldn't secure his release.

"Yes, but you did drive the getaway vehicle."

"I didn't know it was a getaway vehicle."

"But the circumstances don't make it look that way. The clerk says you took off like you were on a drag strip, and the tracks—from your tires, without question—are right there on the road as evidence. How am I supposed to prove you weren't in this thing from the start?"

"Look, I already told you every detail. They egged me on to race away from there. I didn't know why. But when I found out what they had done, I dumped them immediately. I didn't want any part of it."

"Uh-huh. You just happened to wait until you got all the way back to town, and then you 'dumped' them right in front of Roger's house. That sounds like you were real teed off. And what about those two six-packs—from the store—that were still in the backseat of your car?"

"I didn't know they were there, and they didn't find any of the money on me. My hands never touched the gun."

"Jerry," the brown-suited lawyer said as he held his hands out, "if what you're saying is true, you should have reported it to the

police immediately. All I'm telling you now is that you'd better prepare yourself for a rough trial."

Rough was an understatement. Jerry was indicted, tried, con-
victed, and sent to state prison for three to five years. Many people thought it was an unreasonably harsh sentence for a first
offender. But after all the riots earlier that year, Waterston in the
fall of 1968 was intolerant of crime.

But strangely, Jerry seemed to take it in stride. He sometimes
wondered why being in prison didn't bother him more. He was big
enough that he was usually left alone by the other inmates. Of
course, he didn't like being locked up. He'd rather have been out,
working on his car or dating, but he wasn't as depressed as some
of the other prisoners. To him it was just time, not that much worse
than living at home, and he didn't really have any plans or goals for
his future. He read car magazines, watched a lot of TV, and went
out for the prison football team.

The recreation director was a former high school coach with a
five-year-long winning record. But there had been a scandal involv-
ing a high school girl. Parents got together and saw that he was not
only fired but blackballed. The only job he could find after that was
as recreation director for the state prison.

"What's the matter with you, Cox?" Coach Mattson asked after
the second week of training. "Why didn't you go on to college? Why
didn't you play ball?"

"I dunno. Didn't think I was good enough."

"That's your problem. You don't think you're worth anything. I'm
going to start you as a halfback."

"Halfback? I've never played halfback. I was always a fullback
in high school."

"But you're not quite big enough, are you?"

"No. But neither can I cut and slash like a halfback."

"Maybe not. But you can improve. Besides, you have pretty good
speed and a lot more power than's expected of most halfbacks. This
year we've got a line that can open some holes. I need someone
who can go right through them."

Football in the prison was primarily intramural. But there were
two games near the end of the season with teams from other pris-

ons. The respective wardens permitted it—if only because it boosted morale.

The team from Jerry's prison won both games, and Jerry was named MVP.

"What are you doing when you get out, Cox?" asked the coach.

Jerry shrugged. "I don't know."

"Well, I know what you're going to do. You're going to be my ticket out of this place."

"What do you mean? You're not a con."

"I might as well be. I haven't been able to get a job anywhere else for three years. But now I think I might have one sewed up, and you're the thread."

"How's that?"

"You know Tyler, that little junior college over near the coast?"

Jerry nodded.

"There's an old man who financed much of the school on the condition that they maintain a winning football team. This year they've been losing everything. I pulled some strings and got three of the college board members to attend our last game. I've got 'em convinced that if I can bring you, I can turn their team around."

"What about a parole? How will I get out?"

"We've got six months to work on that."

"But, Coach, what if you got me out and then I let you down?"

"You do, and you'll be right back here in prison."

"No. I don't mean that. What if I can't deliver on the gridiron? I've never played college ball."

Coach Mattson looked sideways at him. "Jerry, I've coached a lot of men, and you are one of the best players I've ever seen. You won't let me down."

Tears filled Jerry's eyes. For the first time in his life someone had told him he could be somebody, do something. Maybe he *could* make something of himself. Maybe after junior college . . . university, then the pros.

The coach was still talking. "But first we've got to work on getting you out."

As a result of the coach's efforts, Jerry received an early hearing and was granted parole . . . provided he remained under the personal supervision of the coach for the next two years.

Tyler lost the first game the next season. "I don't know, Coach," Jerry said. He was the last one out of the locker room that night. "What if we don't make it?"

"Don't worry, Son. They can't put you back in the slammer if you keep your nose clean."

"But what about you?"

"Listen. You did fine tonight. We'll pull it off."

In the next game, Coach Mattson started running Jerry on a short-pass pattern across the middle. The opposition wasn't expecting that from a halfback, and Jerry was open every time he tried it. It got the team short but certain yardage, and they won the game.

Tyler lost only one other game that season and went on to take the conference championship. The newspapers regularly credited Jerry as the star, and soon university scouts started offering him full scholarships.

"Cox," Coach Mattson said, "I appreciate your loyalty, but if you want to go with one of these universities, just say so. I'm sure I can arrange some kind of long-distance 'supervision' to satisfy the court."

Jerry decided against it. He was certain, by then, that he wanted to play pro ball, so it was a bit of a risk to stay at Tyler another year when the experience and exposure on a university team might gain him a lot more attention by the pros. But he still felt a little insecure.

Being the star of the football team did something else for him, though. Girls began throwing themselves at him. He didn't even have to try. They were always there, asking if he would take them out or come over to their apartments or go for a ride. Jerry loved the attention; he'd always been rather invisible at Cascade High. He began sleeping around, brushing away twinges of conscience over using girls as playthings. After all, he reasoned to himself, they're just using me as a status symbol and, after all, I'm young only once.

It was nice being the big frog in a small pond. But even beyond the girls, staying at Tyler did not disappoint Jerry. After they had won the first six games in their second season, the coach drew Jerry aside before the next game. "There are some scouts here tonight, so do your best, Cox."

Jerry grinned. "I will, Coach." But what Jerry didn't know was that the scouts were not from a university. They were from the pros. After the game two men approached him and asked if he'd be interested in entering the draft for the next season. Something exploded in Jerry's mind. He was going to make it. He was in.

"Not quite yet," his coach cautioned later. "Being drafted isn't the same as making the team. I'm sure you've got it in you, but it might be wise to get a little more experience first."

But Jerry was as good as on the plane. He was picked as an eighth-round draft choice. He signed without quibbling over salary and went off to training camp in the spring.

The next three years were a whirlwind for Jerry. Not only were the sport groupies offering themselves to him all the time, he was offered promotional deals and asked to make nonprofit fund-raising appearances.

He discovered he had relatives he'd never known existed, calling him up and wishing him well and commending him on some play they'd seen the week before on TV. But sooner or later they got around to reminding him, "Don't forget me, now that you're so famous"—whatever that meant. He figured it meant money. He bought his mother a new house. He felt funny spending that kind of money on her considering the little concern she'd given him as a kid. But then all the guys seemed to be doing that. It was not cool to forget good ol' Mom. Besides, it seemed like he had money to burn, and each contract doubled the salary of the one before.

After his third season, Jerry decided to drive his Porsche 911 back to Waterston. His mom still lived there, but he wasn't as interested in seeing her as in seeing his hometown, the old high school, and maybe some old friends. *I wonder whatever happened to Diana Slater*, he thought as he sailed down the highway in a light spring rain. *She was voted "Most Likely to Succeed." I bet no one ever thought I'd succeed.* But down inside a quiet worry troubled him: When was the party going to end? "Who knows?" he said aloud. "But 'til then, I'm gonna 'keep on dancin', gonna twist and shout.'"

Although Jerry appears to represent an average Joe who never amounted to anything in high school and was expected to live a mediocre life, we can see that he is a very talented individual. This story was taken in part from my client files of the early days of a rather famous professional football player. In high school he, too, was just an average Joe.

If we reflect on Jerry's background, we realize that some elements needed to develop positive self-esteem were missing. Nothing in Jerry's earlier years felt significant to him. No one appeared to believe in him, and he did not accomplish any task of which he was proud.

It's important in the first stage of one's career development to experience some noteworthy accomplishment based on effort, commitment, and drive. Such an accomplishment authenticates the person's existence and says, "You can make a difference; there is a purpose in your life." But in Jerry's case, it wasn't until after high school—when he was at the bottom of the barrel—that anyone saw potential in him. The prison football coach lifted him up and showed him that he could count for something. Jerry was uncomfortable with this new role because it was so foreign to his earlier experience. He almost didn't believe his success was happening and wondered how long it would last. Unfortunately, he continued to have difficulty accepting the fact that he was gifted, that his life could count for something.

Jerry's story also points out how important parents, teachers, pastors, and coaches are in the lives of young people. Someone who believes in a kid and puts his or her neck out for a youth makes an indelible impression that can change the rest of the person's life. It is that "believer-in-them" that the young person remembers when he's down. That significant adult gives the youth the extra boost to keep going when times are rough.

In the next stage of Jerry's career development, it will be important for him to believe in his attribute strengths, take ownership of them, and apply them. He also will need to set realistic goals for the long haul. Otherwise he will flounder as he jumps from one offer to another.

Evaluating the Results

Meeting a client around the age of thirty or shortly thereafter, I find a mind-set very different from that of younger people. This person often comes to me with a desire to take another look at the direction he or she is heading. By this time a lot of major decisions have been made: what to study in school, a career direction, whether and whom to marry. Nevertheless, I find many adults correctly asking, "Am I going down the right path? Is it working out? Is this really what I want to be or do for the rest of my life?"

Surprisingly, a physiological factor underlies the reason for this evaluation phase. Physicians tell us that at about age thirty our bodies peak, and we begin to lose that boundless energy that makes things happen by sheer determination when we're younger. That means we don't bounce back as quickly from doing tasks that are contrary to our natural strengths. During phase two, people find themselves evaluating the results of their first efforts and deciding whether to renew their efforts in that direction or make changes.

The following chapters follow our five travelers, who are now thirtysomething, as they navigate this evaluation phase. As you read, consider whether they recognize what is happening. How successful is their evaluation? What factors influence their decisions? Do these pressure points and/or opportunities sound familiar to you in your thirtysomething years?

As you reached this phase of life, what were your conclusions? Did you make some changes or did it seem best to dive back in and renew your earlier efforts? What was the outcome?

Perhaps you have not yet reached this phase. You may find it hard to believe that your passion to do whatever you set your mind to will be challenged by a body that is declining in strength. Read ahead to see what I have observed in the lives of many thirtysomething clients.

Chapter

Living Up to Expectations

Robert Wilford

After eight years of marriage, Robert found himself coming home from his long days at Wilford Electronics to an increasingly unhappy wife. One night he found Beth sobbing.

"I just can't take it anymore, Robert. I never know when you will be home. Your daughter hardly even knows you." It was the same issue for the last five years.

Again, as he had many times before, Robert tried to appease her, to promise to get home earlier . . . anything to get her to calm down. Finally, she blurted, "The only thing I've ever gotten out of Wilford Electronics is the paycheck you bring home . . . "

"And that's none too shabby," he interrupted.

"Yeah, but I don't even have any close friends in the company. Rachel Macalester's my best friend, and she's from church. But you wouldn't understand that."

"What do you mean, I wouldn't understand?"

"A friend, Robert, a real friend. You wouldn't understand what it's like to have close friends."

"I've got hundreds of friends. You're the one who doesn't like to meet people."

"You've got hundreds of acquaintances, not friends. There's a difference. You don't even let me know what's going on inside you. Sometimes I don't think you even tell yourself."

The accusation bewildered Robert. What was she talking about? He realized that he ought to become more involved in their church. Maybe he ought to deepen his friendships with some people, and the church people would be a good place to start. He actually did attend church whenever he was in town, more out of obligation than because of any faith commitment. And part of the obligation was that he had even been elected to the board of elders. That made him feel a little guilty whenever he thought about it, but then he hadn't asked for the position.

To Robert the discussion seemed to be just another round of Beth's well-worn justification of her apparent coldness to people and dislike of social situations, which clashed with his easy popularity. He was tired of telling her to "get with the program" when they went to social gatherings. He did not understand that she preferred a few close friends to a multitude of casual acquaintances. As a gregarious, outgoing person, he got lots of affirmation for being "friendly," so he easily assumed that he was right and Beth didn't know what she was talking about.

By the time Robert got to work the next day, he had forgotten the conversation with Beth about friends. The problem, in his mind, was Beth's, not his. His father called him into his office and announced that he was promoting him from regional sales manager to vice president of marketing and sales. In that position, Robert would be responsible for recruiting and managing the whole sales team. "The team has grown large enough that it needs special attention, more attention than I can give it. And the first thing I think you ought to do is divide the southwest region and hire another person. But there I go telling you what to do. You're the vice president. You decide what needs to happen."

Robert reviewed the sales records and looked at the amount of territory that needed covering and agreed that another salesperson was needed—but he never seemed to get around to hiring anyone. Finally, Philip Stewart, the southwest regional salesman, came to him and suggested he hire another salesperson.

"Dad recommended that last spring," said Robert, "but I didn't want to cut into your territory."

"It won't hurt me any. I've got far more than I can do as it is, and it will be good for the company."

"What if I moved Gentry over and gave his territory to Roberts?"

"Oh, I don't want Gentry that close. He's not pulling his own weight. I thought you would have seen that and done something about it by now. Besides, that would make Roberts's area too big to cover well."

"Well, I'll see what I can do."

But Robert had a hard time bringing himself to set up any interviews. In his previous years as sales manager he had always deferred to his father for final hiring decisions. Down deep he knew his first choices were not always best. He had files on two or three candidates, but he finally realized that he didn't know how to conduct an interview. He was afraid of making a mistake. As successful as he was at making new friends, he was not good at judging character. He would sit at his desk for long periods of time trying to rehearse what he would say and wondering how he could tell if the person could perform the necessary tasks. How would he know whether the applicant could do what the résumé claimed?

As the days went on, he read some books on management and interviewing. One book had sample questions. "But those questions all seem so plastic. How will I know? How will I know?" he muttered to himself.

Finally, he called in the four candidates whose résumés looked best. They all seemed good. He got along with each one perfectly. He agonized over the decision for days and finally decided that he would hire the first one who gave him a follow-up call. He didn't know whether that meant the person would be more aggressive in sales or whether the person was just more desperate for a job. But when the first person called ten days after his interview, Robert said yes and held his breath.

To his credit, Robert realized he was flying blind. He had no idea how to manage the other people on the sales force, and it scared him. That's when he went to his father and said he wanted to go back to school and get his master's degree in business administration.

"What do you need that for?" his dad asked.

Robert was reluctant to admit how out of control he felt. Maybe that was the way everyone managed, but he didn't think so. "I just think I could do a better job for the company," he said. "Besides, it might really strengthen us. A lot of middle management people are getting MBAs these days."

"Well, maybe. But I think experience is the best teacher. Why don't you give it a chance? You're doing fine. Just do what I tell you."

But there was another reason school looked attractive to Robert, a reason he didn't consciously realize. School was manageable. He knew he could succeed there; he could keep things in control. It felt safe. On the other hand, his father, talented in sizing up job applicants and getting the most work out of employees, had grown up in his work by on-the-job intuitive development. Robert, lacking the natural talents, could not benefit as much from this job experience training process.

However, four months later, it looked like the new man was working out, and Robert postponed his plans for graduate school.

As time went on, Robert tried to spend more time at home, but his new responsibilities as vice president meant more travel to conventions and trade shows. Besides, at home Beth was getting harder to understand. So much of the time she was sharp in her comments, like she was angry with him over something. When he would ask if she was upset, she would answer no. But he still felt uncomfortable.

This unresolved conflict carried over to their sexual relationship. Again Robert was mystified at his wife's coldness to his sexual advances. Understanding his wife's concerns—or anyone's motives for that matter—was becoming a continual problem area for Robert.

Then one day he went to Dallas for a seminar on direct-mail techniques, where he didn't know anyone else. He went up to his hotel room after dinner thinking he would just spend the evening watching TV, but a woman he had noticed several times during the seminar was having trouble getting into the room next to his.

"I can't seem to get my key to work," she said as he passed. "Have you had any trouble with yours?"

"No, mine works fine," Robert said, noticing that up close she was even more attractive than she had been across the room during the day. "Here. Want me to give it a try?" She surrendered her key and stepped aside. Robert slid the key into the lock, and it turned without a hitch. "There you go." He swung her door open for her.

"I can't thank you enough," she said with an infectious smile and a slight blush. "I didn't want to go all the way down to that front desk again. I can't wait to kick off these heels and relax."

"No appointments tonight?" Robert knew there was potential in his question. But it was also the kind of question that could be entirely innocent. He could divert it without embarrassment no matter what she answered.

"No appointments," she said. "I'm stuck alone down here for three days at this seminar that I didn't want to come to in the first place."

She had taken it to the next round. "Me, too," he said. "I was just going to watch TV." He looked sheepishly down at the floor, using the opportunity to peruse her figure inconspicuously. *One might say*, he thought to himself, *that she is very well appointed.* He let the humor of the idea of someone being "furnished" with the best of everything show through as a big smile when he looked up at her again.

"Well, my TV probably gets the same channels as yours; want to watch together?" she offered.

Robert couldn't believe what she was saying. He ought to say no. Instead, he said, "Sure," as he ushered her into her room and shut the door.

"Sit down," she offered as she kicked off her heels. "Want some room service?"

Then Robert heard the faint ring of a phone. It came again, and he realized it was from his room next door. *These walls sure aren't very thick*, he thought. Then he looked at his watch. "Oh, no. That call's for me. I was expecting someone to call at eight." He jumped up and ran out of her room, fumbled with the key in his door, and just made it to the phone on the sixth ring.

It was Beth. They talked for several minutes, and finally Beth said good-bye. Robert realized his mind had been too preoccupied to respond well to her.

Now the spell was broken. There was no need to go back. But then he thought to himself, *She is there and seemingly quite willing.* Not wanting to think too much about what he was doing, he got up, left his room, and knocked on her door.

"Who is it?"

"Me," he said as quietly as possible.

"Come on in." He cautiously opened the door. "I'm just taking a shower," she called as he heard the water turn on.

At the end of the three-day seminar, they arranged to meet in two weeks. And then there was a third rendezvous when Robert told Beth he had to meet Philip Stewart in Santa Monica, California. But while he was gone, their daughter, Alice, became seriously ill and went to the hospital for an appendectomy. When Beth called Philip Stewart to get a message to Robert, Philip had not heard from Robert.

Frantic, Beth contacted the agent who handled the company travel. When he finally realized it was an emergency, he revealed that Robert had flown to Las Vegas and had reservations at the Sands Hotel, room 813.

A woman answered the phone: "There's no Robert Wilford here," she said. "You must have the wrong number." But in the background, Beth clearly heard Robert's voice say, "Who's calling for me?"

"Wait," Beth yelled into the receiver. "This is an emergency. It's about his daughter." She was frantic that the woman would hang up.

After a long silence, Robert came on the line.

When Alice was home and on the way to full recovery, Beth said, "Our marriage has been rough for a long time, Robert, but this is the last straw. I'm leaving." She said it in such a matter-of-fact manner that Robert couldn't even argue.

In all honesty, he did not know what had been so rough about their marriage before his affair. To him it had seemed tolerable enough. But as he thought about losing Beth, he couldn't imagine it. He said, "I love you, Beth. Is there anything I can do to convince you that this won't happen again?"

"Nothing that I can think of at the moment, Robert."

How could all of this have happened to him, the guy who had it made, who was envied by all? Early in life he had achieved what many people work years to get. Now it was falling apart.

After Beth went to live with her mother in her old hometown, Robert's depression got worse by the week. Finally, he went to see the one person he thought could help, the pastor of their church. Slowly, not knowing what to expect, Robert explained the whole situation to him. He was surprised that the older man could really care about him. Up to that time, Robert never really had the occasion to "need" God. Church was a good, wholesome family experience, as it had been when he was a young boy. Robert never thought he was weak enough to need spiritual help. "Is there anything I can do?" Robert asked.

"You have done something just now; you've confessed the whole thing, and that's a good start. But what is it exactly that you want?" asked the pastor.

"I want my wife back . . . I want Alice . . . I want my marriage and family."

"Then maybe the first thing you need to do is confess you were wrong and seek her forgiveness."

But when Beth didn't answer his letters, Robert began to think far more deeply about his whole life. Finally, he decided that if Beth wasn't ready to forgive him, he needed forgiveness from somewhere else. He was beginning to understand that there was an objective wrongness in what he had done, not just that he had been caught and thereby had hurt his wife.

Because of his desperation, he continued to visit regularly with the pastor. Up to this point Robert had sized him up as a teddy bear type who was good only for sermons and handshakes. Robert was amazed at the pastor's insights. He was amazed even more that the pastor cared about him since he had been a distant churchgoer. Through their weekly sessions, the pastor guided Robert to seek forgiveness from God, and in the end, because he had registered years ago as a member of the church, he confessed his self-indulgence to the whole congregation and asked their forgiveness.

Many people thought that making such a sin public was unnecessary, but the pastor disagreed. He tried to show that the demonstration of a changed heart and forgiveness were the signs of a truly repentant person. Robert also discovered something else in the process. He realized that he really cared what God said about his life.

When Beth heard about what had happened, she agreed to meet and talk with Robert.

"I'm not much for theatrics, Robert. If you've done this to get me back, it won't work."

"I did do it to get you back, Beth. But I also did it because now I realize that not only did I hurt you, I sinned against God and the church. I needed their forgiveness just like I need yours. And I am asking you directly: Will you forgive me?"

It wasn't something she could respond to immediately, but three days later she phoned him and said she would forgive him. Then she said, "But there's something I'd like to ask. Can we get some counseling? Things weren't good between us before the affair, and I'm afraid they won't be any better just because we've made up."

Robert agreed.

But the whole process of seeing how far away from God he had been and seeking God's forgiveness caused Robert to remember his mother's long-standing desire for him to become a minister. He didn't really know if that was what he should do, but he wanted to live his life for God—no matter what—so he began toying with the idea of quitting Wilford Electronics and going to seminary.

As he and Beth began to rebuild their relationship, he shared this idea with her. "I'm willing, Robert, if that's what God wants us to do, but it seems like such a switch."

"I know, but somehow working at Wilford Electronics has never been the thing I really wanted to do. I just inherited my position. I never really chose it, and I certainly can't say that God led me into it."

"But who would take over when your father retires?"

"The board will easily find someone. Besides, Dad's not about to retire for several years."

But Robert was wrong. Six months later his father had a sudden heart attack. He recovered, but the doctor ordered him to cut back on his responsibilities. "I'm going to suggest to the board that they make me chairman and promote you to president of the company. I've been getting you ready for this, and now it's time," Robert's father told him.

"But I've been considering some other plans," said Robert, not wanting to let his father down.

"Well? What are they?"

"I've been thinking about going into the ministry."

"Now that's a fool idea. I thought your mother had laid that one to rest years ago."

Once again, his strong, sometimes dominant father took the initiative. It was this ability to see the goal and pursue it while bringing others along with him that distinguished father from son. No matter how much training Robert received, he would never reach his father's level of entrepreneurial effectiveness. Robert's strengths—although clouded by his father's shadow—lay elsewhere.

"Look, Son, you and I both knew this was going to happen some day. It's just come a little sooner than I planned. But you're the man. We need you! I need your help, and this is the time."

"I don't know," said Robert. "I've never felt that comfortable at Wilford. I've always wanted to be in something where I could help people more."

"Help people? You don't know what you are talking about. Just think about it. The company is up to 186 employees now. You'd be helping them. We're one of the largest employers in the town. Now I understand why you haven't felt comfortable in the company. It's an old rule of nature. There just isn't room for two dominant bulls in the herd. Up 'til now, I've been in charge, so naturally you've felt a little restless. That's because we're two of a kind. But now I'm moving on."

But his father's enthusiasm to lay out the red carpet for his son had clouded his ability to objectively evaluate Robert's aptitudes. In his zeal to make his son successful, he had constructed a plan that fit father rather than son.

"I don't know, Dad. I'm not so sure we're all that much alike."

"Sure we are. Everyone in the company loves you. Now, come on. I need you."

As in the past, Robert gave in to the pressure of his father. At the annual meeting the board installed him as president of Wilford Electronics. This pattern of giving in to another's assertiveness would repeat itself.

Robert is now old enough for us to reflect back on his quality of being the "Most Likely to Succeed" that was expressed in phase one of his life. Rarely in the busyness of life do we have the opportunity to follow up on those individuals we knew in high school or elsewhere who seemed to have it all together. In spite of Robert's stereotypical "success image," he, like us all, had his strengths and nonstrengths.

At this point Robert is still confused about what is happening with his life, since earlier everything he touched worked out so well and with so little effort. Those with a multi-relational personality have that to their advantage in their earlier years. They are accepted by people very quickly, but later it can seem that everything in life causes some kind of problem.

He violated his marriage, and he still doesn't understand why he did it, nor does he understand what really makes other people tick. He also has a tendency to be indecisive. He certainly does not have the aggressiveness and entrepreneurial spirit of his father, who built the company. Actually, as we will discover in phase three, Robert has helping talents, which are quite the opposite of his father's Initiating talent strength.

All these tendencies are not uncommon to the experience of many people who demonstrate in phases one and two that surface qualities may not be exactly what is beneath the skin. The factor that causes the most confusion is that in phase two (ages thirty to thirty-five), one still has the stamina and the drive to compensate for talents that may not be naturally present. However, since Robert has passed age thirty, the energy it takes to keep up the image and meet the performance expectations comes with increasing difficulty. Emotional and physical problems can result.

As Robert enters phase three, it is going to be very important for him to come to terms with his strengths and limitations and focus his career and lifestyle around them. Otherwise, he will be headed for some severe disappointments, burnout, and frustration in his marriage.

Chapter

The Vicarious Supervisor

Diana Slater Barber

iana did not attend the seminary wives' club during Jim's final year in seminary. She had an excuse—giving birth to their second baby—but there was more to it than that. She was not about to go back into a situation that had been so hostile. The election incident had been so painful that Diana had become bitter. *If they want to live in the Dark Ages, that's their problem*, she thought.

Actually, Diana had developed a style of responding to established leaders. Because she appeared to be gifted in getting things and people organized (a managing others talent), it was hard for her to be part of any group or committee if it was run poorly. She either took control or quit. With such an otherwise pleasant dispositon, few people noticed this pattern.

As Jim's graduation and ordination approached, he began getting invitations to candidate at several churches in their denomination that were looking for a new pastor. Jim had distinguished himself in seminary, not only with top grades but by preaching whenever possible in local churches. He had put out the word that whenever a pastor was on vacation or wanted a Sunday evening off, he was eager to fill in. As a consequence, he was invited to speak at the denomination's annual conference as an example of the kind of leaders the seminary was producing.

The week of graduation Jim got a call from one of the larger churches in the district—about five hundred members—and was virtually offered a position. It didn't hurt to be recommended by three faculty members.

"This is the chance of a lifetime," said Jim as he got off the phone. "Reverend Jennings is the senior pastor, and they have a full-time youth and music minister, but they want an associate pastor." Diana instinctively responded to a deep concern. Perhaps she hadn't even realized why she spoke up so quickly. The heart of her suggestion was clear to the discerning mind—as a gifted manager, Diana did not want to walk into a confining environment. She wanted free reign to set up the program her way.

"But Jim," queried Diana, "wouldn't it be better to look for a small church that has potential to grow, one where you would be the only pastor, the senior pastor?"

"I don't think so. Reverend Jennings's health is failing, and what he's really looking for is his replacement. If I do well, I'll be given that opportunity. What a chance to serve."

First Church, where Reverend Jennings was the pastor, had a thorough procedure for testing new staff members. For ten days Jim and Diana stayed in a guest apartment of one of the church families. Members of the congregation invited them to meals in their homes noon and evening of every day. The church elders scheduled special meetings to talk with Jim, but he also sat in on all regular leadership meetings. He preached on the first Sunday evening and the following Sunday morning. Then the elders and pastoral staff spent half of Monday with him reviewing what had happened.

Diana's week was just as busy, but she spent more time with the women of the church in their homes—at Monday morning Bible study twice and at a service meeting. She was delighted when they invited her to lead the Bible study on the second Monday morning. The openness to Diana's leadership filled a deep void. Maybe this would work out after all.

"Oh, Jim," she said as they drove back to the seminary, "I hope they call you. This appears to be a much better opportunity than I thought. The women of the church were so welcoming. I think I could really get along well, and there's so much to do. I can't wait to form a committee to work on the church decor. It looks like nothing's been done to it for thirty years, but it could be so beautiful."

By the time they moved, however, redecorating the church wasn't Diana's first priority. She was pregnant with twins, and it was all she could manage to decorate their new home. Their first two children were barely toddlers when numbers three and four arrived. It felt like an instant nursery school.

But the women of the church couldn't have been nicer. The senior pastor's wife treated Diana like a granddaughter, arranging meals after the babies were born and organizing a team of volunteers to do her laundry Tuesdays and Fridays and come in to clean the house on Wednesdays. Someone even took little Tommy a couple mornings a week so Diana could catch up with the twins. Diana felt thoroughly cared for.

In their young family years, Diana poured herself into the home. Raising four little ones was her biggest priority, but she also became a hostess for many meetings and social events in their home. People marveled over how she could manage all she did.

It was managing her home that took up nearly all of her thoughts, energy, and inspiration. Yet, without realizing it, she was polishing some very critical skills in time management and supervision of volunteers.

They had been at the church for eight years when Reverend Jennings announced his retirement and recommended that the church confirm Jim as the new senior pastor. This happened at the annual church members' meeting—though the elders and staff had known of it for a couple of weeks. There was some discussion, then each elder affirmed the direction, testifying to Jim's good service. Bob Fraser, the chairman of the elders board, spoke last. Finally, they took a vote and confirmed Jim as the new senior pastor.

That night in bed Jim said, "It's hard to believe that God has given us this extraordinary responsibility while we're in our early thirties."

"That's true," Diana said as she snuggled closer to him. "But I think you need to be careful of Bob Fraser." Diana wasn't one to be judgmental of others. But once again when it came to issues of power and control, she seemed to have a sixth sense as to who to trust, what to do, and how to do it.

"What do you mean?" Jim recoiled. "He's 100 percent behind me. He's the chairman of the board."

"That's just what I mean. He is the chairman of the elders. I don't know how he worked it out with Pastor Jennings, but he strikes me as the kind of person who takes charge. Now I'm not saying that's bad. I just think the two of you are going to have to stake out new territory." Diana marveled at her own statement. How did she know what she was talking about? She had only attended a few meetings where Bob Fraser was present.

"Don't be silly, Diana. I've been in dozens of meetings with Bob. Of course he takes charge—that's why he's the chairman. But I never saw any standoffs between him and Pastor Jennings."

"Maybe not, but did you ever see them disagree?"

"Sure, from time to time."

"Well, think of an example, and tell me what happened."

"I can't pull an example out of the hat. What is this, a trial or something? No. Wait a minute. I remember one. Just a few weeks ago, when we had decided to buy a church bus to transport the youth to activities, Pastor Jennings wanted to look for a used bus but Bob said we should get a new one. I remember that because I agreed with Bob."

"Well, what happened?"

"I don't exactly know, but it got worked out by the next meeting. There wasn't any big confrontation. Bob didn't insist on his way."

"But we did end up getting a new bus."

"What's that prove? The pastor just came to realize it was a better choice. He's not so stubborn that he can't change his mind."

"No. Of course not. And I'm not saying Bob Fraser always has to have his way. He wouldn't be a good chairman if he did. But he is the president and owner of his own construction company, and it's his nature to take charge."

"Well, what are you saying, then?"

"All I am saying is that with Pastor Jennings out of the picture, it's a new game. You need to take care with Bob Fraser."

Jim did not fully understand what Diana meant, but he tried to follow her advice. Now that he thought about it, this was not the first time she had offered insights into people's personalities. Although Jim failed to realize the major significance of this, her past intuition had proved more accurate than his.

The public school in their part of town was poorly managed. The newspaper often published letters from dissatisfied parents. Diana held Tommy out of kindergarten and then tried to register him in a better school on the other side of town, but the school district was inflexible. "If we let everyone transfer who wanted to, we would have chaos," the clerk said. The private school in town was too expensive.

One day Diana said, "I took several education courses in college: What if I taught Tommy at home, at least until he gets a little older?"

"Diana, we're not out on the mission field, and we're not living a hundred years ago on the frontier. This country established free public schools so mothers could be free from that burden."

"Yes, but I read an article recently that said more and more families are trying it, and the kids learn more and are better adjusted than those in school."

"Well, I don't see how they could learn more at home. A teacher works with her students six hours a day and prepares for the next day's classes in the evening. You couldn't put in near that much time."

"But kids don't need to be in school all day at such a young age. Even as little as two hours a day of personalized teaching is better than all day in a classroom."

So Diana prepared to teach Tommy at home that fall. She ordered books and discovered a newsletter about other families that taught their kids at home. That responsibility, the care of the other children, and being the pastor's wife with all its demands for entertaining kept Diana more than busy.

In the meantime, Jim was busy with a lively congregation. Before Pastor Jennings retired, he told Jim of a new building project for the church. "I'm passing the torch to you, Jim. You're the one who is going to carry it out, and it won't be long before we need it."

Another five years passed before Jim proposed it to the elders. Jim remembered Diana's cautions about Bob Fraser, but so far they had worked out differences easily enough. Still, a new building was a bold suggestion.

Bob Fraser's response was enthusiastic. He had been reading some new reports about how churches grow. "According to some of these researchers," he added, "our church is at the ceiling of what our present facilities can accommodate."

"How can that be?" asked another elder. "We're getting pretty full, I'll admit, but there are always a few empty seats on Sunday morning."

Bob was prepared. "But think about this: Each newcomers' class has twenty to thirty people in it, and we run four a year. But our average attendance on Sunday morning hasn't increased in two years. New people are coming, but they slip out the back door as fast as they come in the front. They feel we don't need them. There's no room."

Jim was delighted. "I think we should appoint a fund-raising committee for a new building."

Fraser suggested mildly, "I think it's better to finance the project and get started right away."

Jim paid no attention and pushed ahead to establish a fund-raising committee.

After the meeting, Bob Fraser stayed until everyone left. Then he said in a firm voice Jim had never heard him use, "Trying to raise the money first is nonsense. I'm a developer and a contractor. These days, nothing gets built that way. It doesn't make sense. At our present size it would take us years to raise that much money. Finance it. When the new building is up and we are twice our size, it will take half the time to pay for it."

"But I think there is a principle involved here," said Jim. "It's not a good idea to borrow . . . "

"Just do it, Jim," Fraser interrupted with a smile. He slapped Jim on the back and headed for the door.

That night as Jim reported the exchange to Diana, his voice got raspy as he shouted, "But I won't do it!"

Diana is quite a contrast from Robert Wilford. Most people who know her well realize that there is much more to her than appears on the surface. Not even Diana knows what it is that drives her to do what she does. Her high school, college, and early marriage years have begun to expose her to opportunities where she instinctively tries to take the initiative but realizes that there are rules of the game that interfere with her ability to take charge. These rules involve the things women are "permitted" to do, what the role of a pastor's wife should be, and other protocol issues.

For now, she is also delightfully saddled with the responsibility of raising her family and managing her household and she is coaching her husband in the pursuit of his career. We are beginning to be aware that coaching her husband is more than just looking out for his interests. It also involves guiding him so she can, through him, get a piece of the action.

As Diana grows older and moves into phase three, it will be very important for her to establish some sphere of responsibility where she can exercise her natural ability to supervise others. If she does not have that opportunity she may, out of frustration, become bitter and perhaps even manipulative of her husband and other people around her.

Chapter 9

Self-Destruct

Phil Grady

Phil noticed Jennifer for the first time on a call to a small grease fire in the restaurant where she worked as a waitress. The cook and manager were nearly hysterical, but the slender, blonde waitress had calmly herded the customers out into the parking lot and was assuring an old woman that everything would be okay.

The grease fire was minor. If the cook had thought to use the extinguisher, he could have put it out with one blast. As it was, black smoke had deposited soot over everything. The place had probably needed a good cleaning, anyway, but the restaurant wouldn't be back in business until the weekend. After ten years in the department, Phil had seen a lot of these grease fires. He felt a sense of pride that he and the truck got there fast enough to prevent a much larger blaze.

"You do this often?" Phil asked the waitress.

"No. Why?" she smiled.

"Well, you handled those people like a pro," Phil said. He waited as the chief talked with the restaurant owner about how to avoid such fires in the future. "You busy tomorrow?"

"It doesn't look like it," she said as she brushed back a wisp of hair with her sooty hand. "At least I hope they don't expect me to scrub walls all day."

"I'll be off at eight in the morning. You want to go to the lake?"

"What? We don't even know each other."

"Sure we do. You're Jennifer," he said as he craned his neck to read her name tag. "And as you can see"—he fumbled with his heavy fireman's coat that hung over his arm to reveal his name tag—"I'm Phil, Phil Grady, actually."

"I suppose I could go to the lake. What time?"

"How 'bout ten?"

"Want me to pack a picnic?"

"Great. See you at ten." He started toward the pumper truck that was ready to pull away. "Hey," he wheeled around, "where do you live?"

Jennifer pulled out her order pad and scribbled her address on the back of a blank check. "See ya tomorrow." She handed it to him as he turned to run and catch the truck.

The next morning he was in his car at 8:01, heading for home to get ready, when he suddenly realized he couldn't remember what he had done with Jennifer's address. He checked his shirt pockets and then nearly drove into a parked car while he fished for it in his pants pockets. "What did I do with that thing?" he wondered aloud. Unable to find the slip of paper, he made a U-turn and went back to the station. Maybe it was in his locker.

When he got there, he checked everywhere.

"You should have an address book like this one," said one of his buddies as he pulled a little black book from his shirt pocket and waved it in the air.

"Yeah, yeah. I know: 'A place for everything, and everything in its place.' You've probably got the names and addresses of all the single girls in the city in there."

"You bet. That way I never have your problem. How much will you pay me for the address of this waitress you're looking for?"

"Forget it. You don't have her address."

"Got a lot of other nice girls in here, though."

Phil stormed out of the station and headed for his apartment.

He found Jennifer later that morning by first going to the restaurant. The manager was there supervising the cleanup. It took a lot of persuading, but Phil finally got him to reveal Jennifer's address.

Phil was twenty minutes late picking her up, but she forgave him, and they had a great day. In fact, that date was the first of many that led to their finally getting married. Perhaps Phil would have married earlier; there certainly were enough available girls he knew, but the thought of being tied down kept him single until he met Jennifer.

For a while Phil's life seemed full and exciting. It was better than he ever dreamed. He had married a beautiful girl and loved coming home where he could kick off his shoes and just relax. He finally felt like he was going to make it in life. He still felt the frustrations of the regimentation at the station and occasionally complained to Jennifer with comments like, "Boy, the fire chief sure doesn't like anybody trying new and different things. I wonder what it's like living at home with him?" But his job seemed tolerable, and he was not aware that his statement had any deep significance.

Still just over thirty, he had the emotional reserve to put up with a job that did not fit his aptitudes and, in fact, stifled his creativity. With his new marriage, some of that coping energy would be used up, yet the need for security and the pattern set by his childhood environment continued to determine his actions.

One day a notice went up on the bulletin board announcing a newly forming firemen's jazz band. Phil eagerly signed up and went back over to his folks' house to find and dust off his old trumpet from high school days. The band was a good outlet for him, because it was the only time when everything wasn't so structured, so straight, so set. He could improvise, adapt, and experiment. But within a year the jazz band fizzled and so did the joy Phil had found in it.

As newlyweds, Phil and Jennifer had both worked and had plenty of money, even when Jennifer cut her hours so she could have more time with Phil when he was off duty. But after their first two children came, Jennifer no longer worked outside the home. They purchased a larger house to accommodate their growing family, and money became very tight.

"Don't most of the other firemen have side jobs?" Jennifer asked one day when they were fretting over finances.

"Yeah. I've been thinking about starting a landscaping business. I'd like to do something sorta creative," Phil said.

With forty-eight hours off after being on duty for twenty-four, Phil had plenty of time to develop a side business. And if they didn't get a night call, the firemen usually got decent sleep while on duty. It was ideal. One of the guys did house siding; another did gutters. Phil finally decided to try landscaping.

He went into debt to buy a truck and a tiller. He read books on landscaping, and for the first couple of months things went well. But then the business began to founder. Phil liked to get his hands in the dirt; he liked working with plants, but he was always experimenting and tinkering with new designs. Soon his customers began complaining because he never quite finished a job, and most jobs ended up costing him more to do than he had originally bid.

"I don't know how you can make any money in this business, anyway," yelled Jennifer one day. "Your tools are scattered all over the garage or out in our yard. Some days you go off without stuff I know you need."

This was a side of Phil that Jennifer had not seen previously. Always before he had appeared orderly, but that was because he was in an environment that required it. Now under the stress of his new business, he was showing his true nature. It took extra effort to put things away and keep them orderly, and Phil just didn't have a lot of extra energy these days. His creative nature was butting heads with the need for orderliness.

"Why can't you get organized, Phil? I go over to the station and everything is absolutely spotless, but around here you're totally lost. You drop things wherever you finish using them and then you forget where they are. The business is going down the tube because you can't get yourself together."

"I am together!" Phil shouted. "And the way I behave in my house is my business." He raked his arm across the top of his dresser to emphasize his point, flinging everything to the floor.

"Stop it!" screamed Jennifer as she ran from the room.

Suddenly Phil was ashamed of himself. He didn't know why he had done it. Recently, Jennifer had nagged him about putting his stuff in the right place, but this was the first time she had really unloaded, and it was the first time he had done something so irrational and spiteful. He didn't know what to do. He felt like life was closing in on him. There was no place he could be himself. Everyone expected him to do things according to some rule book.

He looked at the mess he had made in the bedroom. He really didn't want to hurt Jennifer, so he forced himself to stoop down and begin picking things up. The broken jewelry box weighed a ton, and each tie tack and cuff link eluded his clumsy fingers. His head swam as he grabbed his brush and books. He could hardly stand up. He returned everything to the dresser top and then sat down on the edge of the bed with his head in his hands and sobbed. He didn't know why.

The financial pressure of making payments on his new equipment, the angry customers, and now his own wife. He had always considered himself a pretty easygoing guy, but he sure didn't feel like it anymore. What was happening to him?

In the days that followed, Phil thought a lot about his job. He knew it was a good job—a very good job, most people would say. And there way no way they could afford for him to quit—not now, anyway. But somehow he felt he couldn't take it any longer. He didn't mind the fire calls. He liked the excitement, but he felt suppressed whenever he had to put things away the "right way." He kept thinking of different ways to arrange things. But there was only one authorized way. To get out of the station, he had volunteered to go to schools to tell kids about fire safety or make inspections of buildings—anything to avoid the tedium.

Over the years it had been catching up with him, and now he felt overwhelmed. "What's wrong with me?" he asked himself. "Everyone else seems able to cope, to fit in with the routines, but I can't take it." His one retreat—the place where he could be himself— had been home. He knew Jennifer didn't like it, but he had needed the freedom. And now that was evaporating.

That night Jennifer slept on the couch in the living room, and all the next day she wouldn't speak to him. He could hardly contain the rage that built within him. She put out dinner but didn't sit down with him and the kids.

After dinner, Phil went out to work on his pickup in the long summer evening. Maybe doing something practical would help him feel better, and the pickup needed new brakes. He jacked up the left front wheel and went in the garage to find the safety stand. "Where is that thing?" he asked, slinging stuff aside as he looked for it. Finally he gave up and went back out to the truck.

As he was pulling off the wheel, he remembered that the next day at the station there would be a state inspection. More Mickey Mouse details, he thought to himself. "A place for everything, and everything in its place." Suddenly, Phil was overwhelmed with how deeply contrary that slogan was to his very nature.

The brake drum stuck on the hub. Phil beat at it with a hammer with no success. Then he wedged his jack handle behind the drum and tried prying the drum loose. It gave a little as he pulled, but he couldn't get enough leverage, so he sat down and slid his legs under the car where he could really haul back on the bar.

With the first yank the brake drum popped and started to break loose. He repositioned the bar on the other side of the drum and pulled even harder.

Suddenly, there was a groan and screech of bending metal, and the jack started to tip. The truck was turning over on him! Phil scrambled to get out, but the vehicle crashed down on his feet and lower legs.

He shrieked with pain and then passed out.

Phil awoke to a siren and the sway of the ambulance on its way to the hospital. He was looking up at one of the medics from his own station. "Hey, man. What's happening?" he mumbled.

"Well, Jesus taught Peter to walk on water. You better hope he can help you walk on hamburger."

Phil tried to smile, then drifted back into the darkness.

In the next few days, he was in surgery three times. Finally, after he had been in the hospital two weeks, his chief came in to see him.

"The doc says there's good news and bad news," the chief said. "He says you'll walk again, but he doesn't think you'll ever be able to take the physical strain required for firefighting."

"But don't worry, Phil," the chief reassured him. "If there's one thing the department always does, it's look out for its own. We'd hate to lose you, Phil; you've been a good man. So don't worry; everything is going to work out. I found you a desk job as a dispatcher. Old Hutchinson's agreed to early retirement. What do you think of that?"

Something snapped inside Phil. With the dispatcher's job came paperwork. The whole job was nothing but filling out forms, filing reports, and keeping things in order. There wouldn't even be any fires to go to. He tried to say thanks, but the words just wouldn't come.

A few days later his doctor said, "It's normal after an injury like this to go through a time of depression. I think you'll do best at home, and there's no real reason for you to remain in the hospital. You can just come in for your therapy."

"You think I'm depressed, Doc?"

"Yes, I do. You're showing every sign of it. But don't worry, you'll be back on your feet pretty soon," and then he laughed at his own pun. Phil did not think it was funny.

The hospital released him that afternoon.

Back at home, Jennifer was glad that Phil was recovering and tried to be nice to him because of his injury, but the problems they had faced before the accident had not gone away. If anything, the depressed Phil was harder to live with than he had been before the accident.

One day while he was yelling at her for putting his socks in his drawer where "I can't find them. I thought they were right here on this chair," Jennifer dropped the rest of the laundry in the middle of the floor and yelled back. "Phil, I've had it. I don't care whether you've been injured or not. I'm taking the children and leaving. In fact, I want a divorce!"

She had left by the middle of the afternoon.

At this point in Phil's life we are beginning to see a pattern that, as he grows older and moves into phase three, will become even more pronounced: the incongruity between his job duties and his natural talents.

In Phil, I've selected one of the most classic talent incongruities, since it comes up so often in my clients. This talent conflict impacts one's self-worth, one's marriage, and ultimately one's identity.

To understand this talent conflict, let's recall that back in phase one, Phil was fairly comfortable with himself and his surroundings. There was nothing really outstanding about his background, but nothing really that negative, either. Following high school, he went into the military and, because of his youthful zeal and strength, he did not find any unusual conflicts with what he was expected to do. Now in phase two, however, it is possible to see that there was a struggle growing inside Phil from his youth onward.

We find that he is a very creative person. That means that he constantly seeks new and different ways to do things and does not naturally appreciate routine, established traditions, or policies and procedures. His personality leads him to challenge the idea of "a place for everything, and everything in its place."

Because his parents' home was a highly structured environment, Phil developed the habit of orderliness and mistakenly assumed it was a part of his nature. The military and even his job in the fire department affirmed his assumed orderliness, but as Phil grows older, his tolerance for the structured life is diminishing. He no longer has the energy to put up with such demands. Deep down he is still seeking a way to be himself. Phil represents many individuals who, in phase two, are still longing for the place where they fit into the world.

Getting married and having children are two developments that use a lot of energy, energy Phil had once used to cope with his structured environment. As we watch him move into phase three, it will be important for him to come to an honest understanding of how he is gifted and try to develop a balance in his home and job that affirms his strengths rather than puts demands on his areas of non-strength. In short, he needs to find an outlet for his innate creativity. If Phil doesn't turn things around in phase three, then his work, as well as his overall life, will start to go downhill at a rapid pace.

Chapter

Taking the Big Risk

Claire Winters Sorenson

S etting up house with David Sorenson was no picnic. Claire had not accumulated many things, and David had allowed his former wife to take most of his household items, so Claire and David had to shop together to furnish their new condominium.

They were alike in the joy they got from analyzing ideas or literature, and they both were fastidious people, but the details David cared about were numbers and facts and managing his time efficiently. The details that were important to Claire, on the other hand, were having places to put things. Her sense of orderliness was the complete opposite of Phil Grady's creativity. Everything had to have its place and its policy. Routine and consistency were high priorities.

While shopping, David watched their money as well as the time it took to make a decision. He had a built-in clock that allowed him to be naturally efficient with time. Claire went more slowly, trying to figure where things would fit and how they would look. "Don't rush me," she protested. "We can't just fill our place with clutter. I'm not going to buy something until I'm sure it is right for our home."

They made it through the process, but it left Claire a little shaken. David never said anything about his former wife, but Claire couldn't help wondering how she compared to her in this as well as many other areas . . . including her looks. She concluded that such insecurities were inevitable when a second marriage was involved.

And she was right. Claire's insecurities about David's former marriage was one reason their marriage relationship developed cautiously. But Claire was also the kind of person who warmed to new relationships slowly. Throughout her life she had cultivated only a few "best friends." David was one of them, but developing marital intimacy with him was a much more intense venture.

One day she mentioned it in a letter to her friend Esther, who had found the teaching position she wanted—all the way across the country. Still, they kept in regular contact with each other by mail. "I'm not one for sappy romances," wrote Claire, "but I thought David and I would be a lot closer by now. Instead, it's more like the good old times when the three of us were together: just great friends— except, of course, that we sleep together. Maybe I shouldn't complain. I guess there are a lot of married couples who find that nothing's left when the fiery passion dies down. At least I have hope we'll be rocking-chair friends."

Esther wrote back: "Don't give up. My mom and dad's marriage was almost an arranged one, but they were well matched for each other. Mom used to say that romance will come if everything else is right. And, though it may have taken longer, I think they loved each other more deeply than anyone I've ever known. I only hope I have a marriage as good."

Understanding herself in terms of work was something else that still troubled Claire. One evening after she complained about how she had been treated at work, David suggested, "Well, why don't you quit that newspaper job?"

"Oh, it wasn't that bad."

"Still, I earn plenty of money for the both of us. There's no reason for you to have to work there."

"You make it sound like I don't matter. What would I do? I don't want to be just a housewife."

"What's so wrong with that?"

"Nothing. But I didn't get my Ph.D. to keep house."

"Well then, you could write. You've always wanted more time to write."

"Yes, maybe so," Claire's voice trailed off.

"What are you thinking?" David probed.

Claire's mind spun with the prospect of trying her wings in the field that mattered to her most. "I don't know. I just . . . there's not that much wrong at the *Globe*."

"You should give yourself a chance, Claire. Those articles you have written are good. I think you could make it as a writer."

Claire laughed. "Getting a couple of articles published in a local magazine is a long way from being a real writer."

"Don't put yourself down. When you say that kind of thing about yourself, that's the way other people are going to see you . . . and what's worse, you're likely to begin believing it."

Down deep Claire was reminded of why David was so special to her. He really believed in her. It made all the difference in the world. It was just that encouragement that brought her out of self-doubt. "What difference does it make with writing?" she said. "It's only the product that counts."

"Not exactly. Take that paper where you work. For years now you have let them take advantage of you. Sometimes you have to teach people how to see you."

"What? Teach people how to see me? What do you mean?"

"If you don't teach people how you want to be perceived, they will form their own opinions, which may not be that favorable."

"You sound like a PR agent. I don't want to go around tooting my own horn. If other people don't recognize that what I do is valuable, I'm not about to go around 'marketing' myself," she said, but admitting to herself secretly that she did like it when David affirmed her.

"No, no, no. That's not it. Think of it this way: Suppose a bunch of us were planning a party . . . "

"I don't really like parties."

"Just listen to me a minute. You're planning a party. Someone has to plan the food. Someone has to write and send out the invitations. Someone has to decorate the place. Someone has to coordinate cleanup. Which of those things would you like to do?"

"The invitations, I suppose."

"Okay, and let's say you hated planning food for big groups. Now one way you teach people to understand and appreciate your strengths would be to volunteer for the invitations before someone asks you to do the food. That's not tooting your horn; it's just educating them. It's teaching them what you do best rather than waiting for them to guess."

"What's that have to do with writing?"

"At the newspaper, you might look for ideas of things you could write and ask for the opportunity to try. It's having the courage to make the opportunity for yourself."

After that, Claire made one or two feeble attempts at volunteering for writing projects at the *Globe*, but it never went anywhere. Then she and David discovered they were pregnant. Claire set aside her dreams of writing and prepared for the baby.

Six months later, she quit her job at the *Globe*. At first it was scary to give up the security of "what she did," but it was also incredibly freeing.

Then baby Kevin came. The delivery went smoothly, and the boy was healthy. Claire's mother came to help out for a couple weeks, but then she left, and Claire was alone at home all day with a baby who cried and ate and cried some more but never slept as much as Claire would have liked.

Claire's world contracted to diapers and laundry and shopping and cleaning and trying to talk with David when he got home from work. But their worlds seemed to be drifting apart, and in time, she gave up her writing.

Claire hoped that when Kevin got a little older, things would be better. She might have time to start writing again. But when he began crawling and talking he got worse. Once he could get around, he was into everything. He was worse than a college roommate: He never even pretended to ask before pulling open her desk drawers. He dumped every bottle of shampoo into the bathtub one day when she wasn't watching. He "toasted" a plastic record in the toaster. He climbed on top of her dresser—she could never figure out how—and sprinkled her expensive new perfume over everything in the top drawer.

One morning when Kevin was two, Claire took him to the grocery store with her and sat him in the shopping cart. He began to fuss, which Claire tried to ignore. They came around the end of an aisle, and Claire stopped to compare the ingredients on two cake mixes. She turned back toward Kevin just in time to see him leaning as far out of the cart as he could, grabbing at a six-foot-tall display of gallons of apple cider. Claire screamed, and Kevin jumped back, but he did not let go of the cardboard divider between two layers of the jugs. As the display swayed, Claire had presence of mind enough to pull the shopping cart and Kevin back out of the path of the falling tower.

The crash was terrible.

They both were safe, but as Claire stared at the juice flooding down the aisle of the store, her first thought was that it would take forever to clean the sticky stuff from under the counters and displays. Kevin was screaming. Then Claire looked up and saw customers peering around the ends of the aisles. A terrified clerk in a white apron broke through a knot of onlookers and came running toward her.

All Claire could think of was that she wanted out of there. She grabbed Kevin and fled the other way and out of the store, leaving her groceries in the cart surrounded by the golden sea of cider.

Kevin screamed all the way home in the car. Claire felt guilty that she couldn't seem to control him. He was only two years old, but she was completely overwhelmed. Where had her stable, manageable world gone? The house was a mess, and she was trapped in a world that was completely out of control. She put Kevin in his crib, closed the door, and then flopped down on the couch and began to cry. Her sobs came louder and louder until they drowned out Kevin's wails.

There must be something really evil about me, thought Claire as she cried. I think I am beginning to hate him. Sometimes I think I hate David, too, for getting me into this.

She began evaluating her life. She was past thirty. She had a Ph.D., but she wasn't using it. She didn't even work at the newspaper anymore. *Maybe I should have become a teacher like Esther,* she thought. *I could have remained single and made a contribution to the world.* Claire still read literature; she wrote letters to her old friends and sometimes included a verse of poetry that she had composed. But she felt it was a sham. She wasn't a poet; she wasn't a writer. She had nothing to show for her life.

She remembered a year earlier when she had applied for a checking account at their new bank. The bank officer asked, "How do you want your degree noted on your checks? Do you want a 'Dr.' before your name, or do you want a 'Ph.D.' after your name?" Claire remembered that she had hesitated and turned very hot—probably blushing, she recalled. Then she had said, "Oh, I'm not really sure. Why don't you just list my name by itself." In the car, she had broken into tears. "What was it all for?" she had said out loud as she banged the steering wheel.

Again she was overcome with feelings of aimlessness. *I can't go on this way,* she thought. *I've got to do something.*

Claire remembered a brochure that had come by mail from the university. It was for a writers' seminar. She jumped up from the couch and rummaged through the collected junk mail until she found it. The seminar was two weeks away. She would go. Maybe some inspiration, some connection, some opportunity would strike her there. Their neighbor girl had baby-sat Kevin before. This would be a little long to leave him, but he would just have to manage. Claire reasoned that she could sign up like any other beginning writer—after all, that's all she was—and no one had to know about her degree.

Two weeks later, as the seminar was coming to a close, Claire was inspired to try much more seriously to write and sell some articles. The prospect made her feel good again, and then as she was leaving the seminar she ran into her favorite college professor from years before.

"Claire, how's it going?" asked Professor Warner, remembering her name, after five years without any coaching.

They exchanged pleasantries and then she pressed Claire about her writing, and suddenly Claire was blurting out all her pain and frustration about not doing anything with her life.

"Oh," the professor said, "we've got to do something about that. In all my years at the university, you were one of my best students. We can't let you get lost on the shelf. Didn't you used to be interested in the theater?" Professor Warner knew how to affirm a person. She used more "we shoulds" than "you shoulds" in her conversation.

"Yes. I love plays," answered Claire, not knowing what that had to do with her writing interests.

"Well, you're familiar with the *Community Marquee* aren't you?"

"Isn't it that little magazine about community theaters?"

"Yes," said the professor, "but I bet you didn't know it was published right here in town."

"Is it? I thought it came out of New York."

"No. The editorial offices are right over on Barkley Street. I know the editor quite well. Come over to my office."

Once in her former professor's office, all the old excitement of college days came rushing back for Claire. "Here," said her professor, tossing her a recent copy of the magazine. "Now, let me see. I had that number somewhere."

Soon the older woman was dialing the phone, and then she was speaking about Claire: "Yes, you remember you were telling me you needed some good writers? I've got just the person for you. Claire is one of the most gifted writers I've met, and she lives right here in town. How about giving her an assignment? If she does well, maybe you can use her some more . . . Okay, I'll send her over . . . tomorrow afternoon okay?" she said, nodding her head at Claire to see if the time was workable.

Claire nodded back, figuring she would work it out somehow.

"But what if I can't do it?" mumbled Claire after her teacher hung up.

"Don't be silly. You'll do fine."

The first article was nothing more than an annotated list of new plays suitable for community theaters. But the day after Claire delivered it to the editor, she got a call.

"We've had a little problem," the editor started, and Claire's heart sank as she imagined her assignment being rejected, but the editor continued. "My assistant editor has just taken a position at another publication, and we are desperate to get out the next issue. Is there a chance you could help us? We can't pay much, but if you could fill in, we'd be very grateful. By the way, you did a fine job on that assignment."

I did fine on the assignment? Claire thought. *That's good. But what else is this? He wants me to fill in?* "Oh, I don't know how I could do that," she found herself saying into the phone. "I've got a child to take care of."

After a moment's silence the editor said, "Couldn't you get someone to take care of him for a few days? We'll try not to string this out too long."

They don't really want me, Claire thought. *They are just desperate.* "Well, I suppose I could arrange something temporarily."

"Good, good. See if you can come in about noon tomorrow. If that won't work, would you give me a call as soon as possible?"

"Yes. I'll be glad to." And Claire hung up the phone. She already knew who could take care of Kevin.

Those first few days stretched into three weeks and then a month where Claire worked every afternoon. Then one evening Claire complained to David, "They're just using me at that magazine."

"What do you mean?"

"They don't value my writing. They just wanted someone to fill in," she said, hoping he wouldn't agree.

"But you keep telling me that they've been asking you to write various things."

"Sure, but so what? They could hire anyone to do that."

"Not anyone, Claire. They would have to find someone who could write."

"Write?" She rolled her eyes and flung her hand in the air. "They're just using me."

"Claire, that's not the way the world works. You're getting paid, aren't you?" He did not wait for her to answer. "They haven't asked you to leave, have they?"

"No. As a matter of fact, the editor asked me if I'd consider remaining permanently, but . . . "

"But what, Claire? What do you want? Do you have to win a Nobel prize before you realize you have something to contribute?"

Three days later the first issue on which Claire had worked came off the press. She paged through the magazine, remembering things she had written, corrections she had made. There was the comma correctly inside the quotation mark instead of outside. There was the correct date: 1883, not 1884. A tentative warmth of satisfaction settled over her. And then, quite by accident, she turned to the masthead and saw her name listed as assistant editor. It stirred a deep sense of purpose within her. For the first time in her life she had done something of note.

She got up out of her chair and barged into the editor's office without knocking. "I didn't say I could do this," Claire blurted. She stood before him with her finger pointing to the masthead of the magazine.

"Do what?"

"Take the job."

"But you were the assistant editor on that issue, weren't you?"

"Well, I don't know. All I did was help you out."

"Just take my word for it: You were the assistant editor. Now, have you made up your mind about accepting the position permanently? I need to know soon."

Then, from a distant place, Claire heard her voice speaking the words: "Yes, I'd be glad to. I think I can work it out."

As we close phase two of Claire's life, we find that she is still not giving herself much credit for her talents. She is like many people I have met over the years—a very gifted individual who just doesn't believe in herself. Fortunately, in her husband, Claire has a coach who will encourage and prompt her in ways she lacked in earlier years.

Claire is quite different from Phil Grady in that Claire prefers highly structured environments while Phil tends to be creative and innovative. Generally, structured people find it hard to be homemakers with small children who constantly tear things down and mess them up. This will cause Claire a needless amount of guilt if as a mother she wonders why she feels so frustrated. This also will be a drain on her ability to pursue her writing and other career possibilities.

What has occurred for Claire in phase two is the documentation of her attributes when she saw her name in print. Such a validating experience is important when a person is trying to come out from under a toadstool, so to speak. We notice that Claire's insecurity is so severe that she doesn't even believe that what she has done is worth anything. Fortunately, her persistent coach-husband keeps affirming her. It will be very important in phase three for Claire to achieve a major accomplishment demonstrating her natural strengths so that she can rebuild her identity around a sense of purpose and direction.

Chapter 11

Gettin' No Respect

Jerry Cox

Back in his old hometown for the off-season, Jerry Cox kept a pretty low profile. He stayed with his mom—in the new house he had bought her.

His mom wasn't working . . . again. But she kept talking about buying a small motel she could run. Jerry knew it would never happen, not unless he provided the money. He could do that easily enough, but didn't really think she would make a go of it. It just didn't seem like a good idea.

From time to time Jerry tried to contact a few old classmates, but they all seemed to have moved away. On a whim, he even called Diana Slater's folks. "I'm sorry," her mother said over the phone, "she's not here. Could I take a message?"

"I'm Jerry Cox . . . an old classmate of Diana's."

"Oh, yes. Well, how nice of you to call, Mr. Fox. No, Diana's not here. She's married now, you know—to a nice seminarian. Everything's going so well for them. She's finished her degree, and I expect they'll be getting a little church somewhere soon."

"That's great," said Jerry. "Maybe you could just tell her that Jerry Cox called to say hi."

"Oh, Cox. I'm so sorry," the woman laughed nervously. "I thought you said Fox. Of course I'll tell her you called. Did you know her at the university?"

"No. Just high school. Thank you," and he hung up.

A strange mood came over him. It was as though he had never left Waterston . . . never made it in the pros. He was still the high school loser. Everyone else had left him in the dust in their scramble for success. It felt like a bad dream where he was running as fast as he could but couldn't get anywhere. The strangest part was that he had succeeded but nobody knew it.

Then somehow the local newspaper, the *Waterstonian*, got word that he was in town, and a reporter came by and interviewed him. A photographer took some pictures, and Jerry started to feel much better. He was finally getting the recognition he deserved.

But when the paper came out the next afternoon, he could hardly believe what he read: "The last time Jerry Cox was in Waterston, he was on trial for robbery. And the verdict was 'Guilty.' Today, he walks our streets again. . . ." The story then reviewed his mediocre high school career, the robbery—with all the details except those that proved his innocence—and then his life in prison. It was a long feature, "continued on page eight."

Jerry grabbed the phone and dialed. After two secretaries put him on hold, he finally got through to the reporter. "What are you doing to me?" he yelled into the mouthpiece.

"Who is this?"

"It's Jerry Cox, you idiot."

"Hey, Jerry, my man. How you doin'?"

"How am I doin'? What do you mean, 'How you doin'?' You crucify me, then ask how I'm doing?"

"Calm down now and tell me what the problem is."

"You made me out like a criminal. I'm a football star. People all across this country watch me on TV. I get paid more money in one season than you'll see in your whole life. You're the one who ought to be worrying about how you are doing, because when I get through suing that rag of a newspaper you write for, I'll own it. And the first thing I'm going to do is fire you!"

"Jerry, Jerry, we didn't portray you as a criminal. I did talk about your dramatic football success."

"Where? I read four columns and haven't seen the word 'football' once except where you said . . . what was it? I played 'a second-rate game in high school.'"

"Look on page eight, Jerry."

Jerry flipped through the notices for grocery-store specials and the auto dealer ads until he found the rest of the story about himself. He scanned down the column and noticed that the story did end by reviewing his recent football successes. "Yeah, but you buried it at the end. No one will read that far. All they'll get is that I've been in prison."

"Jerry, first of all most people know you are a football star. That's not 'news.' I just wanted to tell the story of how someone can rise from the ashes, so to speak. It's a feature story. I saved the best until last."

Jerry slammed down the phone.

"What's the matter, Jerry?" his mom asked as he stomped through the kitchen.

"I'm getting out of this hick town and never coming back," he grumbled as he hastily packed his sports bag.

His mother came to the door and said, "But Jerry, we're almost ready to eat. I ordered a pizza. It'll be here any minute."

He looked at her, wringing her hands in her apron. "Sure, Mom. I'll stay and eat." He slowed down. After all, it wasn't her fault.

Later that evening as he wheeled his Porsche out onto the highway, he flipped on the radio. It just happened to be tuned to the rock-and-roll station he had always listened to as a kid. But now its nighttime programming was a call-in talk show.

The host was saying, "What about this Jerry Cox, hometown-boy-makes-it-big-in-football? There was an article about him in today's *Waterstonian*. What do you think? 555-6363. We're interested in your views right here on KOJO talk radio. Hello, you're on the air."

"Well, I read about that boy," whined the voice of an older woman, "and I remember when he committed that robbery. It was a terrible thing. You know, I never did like football. It's such a violent sport. But I guess since there are people out there like him, it's good if they can focus their violence in a way that doesn't hurt other people. And it sounds like this boy has finally learned to do that. So I say . . . "

Jerry flipped off the radio and wound the needle on his speedometer up to ninety-five before backing off on the accelerator.

Things were different at his condo in Colorado. There people knew him as a football star, especially the women around the pool. People were always eager to go out to dinner with him. One thing he didn't take much notice of, however—or didn't talk about if he did notice—was that they always seemed to let him pay. But then he was the one with all the money.

Before he had to report for training camp that summer, Jerry took a trip to visit Coach Mattson.

"Tell me how it's going," the coach said in his living room that first evening.

"Great. Couldn't be better," said Jerry.

"No. I'm serious. How's it going?"

"I told you. Everything is going great. I'm playing football, pulling down six figures. I play every game. No serious injuries." He held up both hands with his fingers crossed. "What more could I want?"

"You investing any of your money?"

"Oh, yeah. There's this developer in Florida who's building a big sports complex, and he's putting my name on it. I'm investing a lot of money in that. I should see some good returns."

"Jerry, he should be paying you to use your name, not you paying him. Have you ever been down there to see what this place is like?"

"No, but he has all these plans and drawings. It's a development, you know."

"Plans and drawings are cheap. They don't mean a thing. You'd better get a lawyer to check it out."

A little later Coach Mattson asked, "What are you going to do when your football years are over?"

"Who knows? I'm just getting started."

"Jerry, you know what they say: Time flies when you're having fun. It won't be that long. You ought to think about it."

"Oh, I have, I have. I might go into car racing . . . or something else."

"You have the quick reflexes to race, and you enjoy competition. Might work out. Have you ever driven?"

"We used to drag our cars at night down by the river. We had a quarter mile marked off on a straight stretch of the road. And a friend let me drive his stock car around a dirt track a few times. But no, I've never really raced."

"Well, you ought to think about what you want to do long-term, Jerry. In your game, the future comes real soon."

Three more years passed, and Jerry was at the height of his career. Occasionally, he thought about what Coach Mattson had said, but what could he do?

He decided to get a little more serious about life. He married his live-in girlfriend, Lisa, and made their two-year-old son legitimate. For a while, he kept to one woman. But when he was on the road, with all those beautiful bodies throwing themselves at him, it was hard.

Still, life was good. He was one of the older veterans on the team, and it was his duty to bring a little maturity to the rookies.

Then on an icy Sunday afternoon in December, they were playing the Chicago Bears in Soldier Field. It was third and four, and Jerry was running the crossing pattern guaranteed for some short yardage. He had to jump high to catch the ball, and just when he came down on his right leg, he was hit from the right side at the knee. He heard the snap and knew he was in trouble before he felt the pain.

The paramedics rolled him off the field on a gurney, and he was scheduled for surgery the next day. It was the end of his tenth season, but Jerry was determined to come back. For the next several months he did not miss a single day of therapy. He was late to training camp—he couldn't get the doctor to release him—but he finally made it. The coach didn't play him in the exhibition games, but he let him start in the first regular-season game.

Jerry knew that physically, he wasn't 100 percent and the sound of his knee snapping kept replaying in his head. This led to a rather conservative game on his part, and the team lost. He blamed himself, and so did the papers.

But the next week he felt stronger and was determined to prove the sportswriters wrong. It was not time to hang up his cleats! They won that game, not because of any grand plays by Jerry, but at least he wasn't accused of losing the game for the team.

With each succeeding game that season Jerry felt as if he was getting stronger, but the sportswriters kept speculating on who would take his place when he retired. And in every news conference he was asked whether he planned to be back the next season.

"Of course I'll be back," he shouted. "Why wouldn't I? I have another year on my contract, and I'm playing just fine."

But when it came time for negotiating a contract renewal, the management would not extend him more than one more year, and he could not get the pay increase he thought he deserved. He even put out unofficial feelers to other teams, but the money wasn't there, either.

The next two years, Jerry did not suffer another injury to his knee, but there were a lot of other injuries—separated ribs, pulled hamstrings, broken thumb (twice)—and he started missing more games than he played.

He knew it would soon be over, and he started thinking seriously about Coach Mattson's question: "What are you going to do when your football years are over?"

Like many others who achieve high positions early in life, Jerry had no realization of what it was like to "live in high society." Even though he had been in prison, he'd had nothing to lose at that time. He was just marking time. Now he had made it, and it was hard to face the fact that life was going to change.

Every time the question of what he was going to do after football came to his mind, he thought about his own youth and how there hadn't been anyone to give him the boost he needed. "If it hadn't been for Coach Mattson," he said to his wife one day, "I might still be in prison."

There were always people trying to get him to endorse some product or invest in some venture. Jerry took a chance with first one and then another—always arranged through a friend of a friend—but all too often he lost.

Within six months after retiring from football, his financial assets had been seriously depleted, and he had nothing substantial to show for his football success. Jerry found his mind drifting back to his high school days and the C+ grades that characterized him then. "I feel like I've been a fake for several years, and now they've found me out," he said to Lisa one day when his depression was closing in on him. "We've been living high on the hog, and now we're gonna pay for it."

"I should have known," Lisa replied. "Why don't you go out and get a regular job? At least then you wouldn't be moping around the house all the time."

Then one day Jerry got a call from a man who said he was from a YMCA camp in the Rockies. "I know this is a long shot," the man said, "but would you be willing to come up and spend a week with the boys this summer? It would be an inspiration for them to just talk to Jerry Cox. And any football training you could give them would be great."

Jerry agreed, and when he came back, he thought he knew the answer to Coach Mattson's question. "I'm going to start a sports camp to help kids like I was," he announced to his wife. "We'll do everything—football, basketball, skiing in the winter. What do you think?"

Jerry, like all our other characters, is gifted and comes from his own unique environment. His home, like some of ours, was not supportive, and therefore he interprets himself and the world around him through a cloud of self-doubt. Jerry's coach, who stepped into his life and believed in him in phase one, illustrates how helpful someone can be when he or she believes in another's attributes and helps that person succeed in using those strengths.

Unfortunately, Jerry does not choose to listen to his coach's counsel regarding life after football. Listening to others is critical. If Jerry is to grow beyond his early success as a football player, he will need to understand what brought him to his place of fame and success. He will need to realize that he has other aptitudes he can develop and use. If Jerry builds his entire identity upon his fleeting image as an athlete, he will encounter only disappointment as he grows older. Phase three will be a very critical time for Jerry in establishing and developing his identity for the future.

Although I have worked with a number of professional athletes, this pattern of early fame and success followed by disillusionment is not unique to the sports world. Family businesses and parents who help "set up" their children also foster this typical early-success syndrome.

Confirmation or Collision

I believe that the period between ages thirty-five and forty-five is often the most critical phase of a person's adult development. Here is the opportunity to reevaluate the adjustments made in phase two or, if no adjustments were made, to make some before the person suffers serious health or personal consequences.

In the following chapters, take note of which of our five friends are adjusting to vocations (or avocations) that make the most of their natural talents and strengths, and which ones still seem mismatched. What are the issues affecting their decisions? What are the results of successfully matching inherent strengths with how each spends his or her time? What is the impact on other areas of life when one still hasn't found one's niche by this phase? Are there adjustments that can still be made?

If you have hit this phase, which of the characters represents your current situation? If you have not reached this phase, think of an acquaintance who has. Whom is he or she most like?

Chapter 13

Starting to Come Apart

Robert Wilford

When Robert became president of Wilford Electronics, the employees felt relieved. With the popular young executive in control, the company was in good hands, their jobs were secure, and everyone looked forward to continued success.

Then one day Robert's father called him aside. "Son, now we need to get down to business. I need to tell you a few things about running this company. First, don't trust Greg, my . . . ah, your vice president of finance. He's a good accounting man, but he lacks good judgment. If you don't watch him closely, he could make some very costly mistakes.

"Remember that contract with Central Electric to make those solenoids? It costs us fifty-eight cents to make each one and he almost agreed to sell them for fifty-seven cents. We would have lost a penny apiece, and the company would have lost considerable income if I hadn't caught it. He was so excited to land such a big contract that he hadn't even run the figures. So watch him, or he'll put us under."

The older man frowned thoughtfully. "Second, you're a good, decent person, Robert, and I'm proud of you, but now that you're president, you can't be Mr. Nice Guy. It's lonely at the top; some people are going to think you're mean, but you're not. You're just being tough-minded, doing your job. I know that when you were growing up you wanted people to like you, and they did. I don't know; maybe I made it too easy for you, but sometimes you have to be the tough guy. This might be hard for you, but you have to do it.

"And that brings me to the third thing: Don't be afraid to fire somebody. I've watched you; sometimes when people aren't cutting it, you have a tendency to talk with them too many times, and I've never seen you fire anyone. If you let problems slide, people won't respect you, and they'll start taking advantage of you."

Robert looked a little bewildered when his father ended his speech. "So why are you telling me all this?" he asked.

"To prepare you. Everything is going well now, but sooner or later someone is going to test your mettle."

As Robert walked away, he still did not understand why his father had given him the tough-man pep talk. Nothing had happened to cause this concern. But he found out soon enough.

The next week he was going over the sales reports from each region when he discovered that the report from Jay Miller, the man he had hired to take over part of the southwest region, seemed out of line. First, sales were down. Second, his expense report was unusually high.

Robert called accounting to get the details on Miller's travel. Some destinations were out of his region, and the places he had been staying were unusually expensive.

Then he noticed that the Alta account, one of the largest from that region, seemed to have died about a month before—all orders had stopped. He called the company and was shocked at the story he finally got from the president. "Look, I hate to say this," the man said over the phone, "but your man Miller's style of playing with numbers didn't impress us. Our purchasing people got the impression he was negotiating a below-market price that would be raised after we turned down the competition. We want the best price we can find, but we don't do business that way."

"Why didn't you call me and tell me immediately?"

"Maybe I should have," said the man. "I know we've done business with your firm for years, but I won't put up with this kind of stuff. If you don't know what's going on with your field staff, I'm going to let you have that problem. I sure don't want it."

As he hung up, Robert felt like he had just been caught in a catch-22. One of his clients had dropped him because a salesperson was playing lowball, a practice expressly forbidden. When he cooled off, he realized that as unfortunate as that may be, his real problem was with Miller.

When he called Miller in, Miller had an answer for everything—until Robert confronted him with the report of lowballing the Alta account. Then Miller switched and confessed everything: padding his expense account, even selling some other products freelance while he was on the road for Wilford. But he begged Robert's forgiveness and promised to make it up to the company if only Robert would give him a second chance.

Robert didn't know what to do: He told Miller he needed time to think about it. That night Robert couldn't sleep; he felt sorry for the man, and he reflected on how his wife and church had forgiven him when he had been unfaithful. Didn't the Bible say that we would be forgiven as we forgive others? he reminded himself. Two more days went by while Robert struggled with the decision. He thought about consulting his father, but he knew what his father would say: "Fire him. He has to learn a lesson, and you have to maintain discipline in the company."

Robert just couldn't do that, so he finally gave the man a second chance. He felt good about himself as Miller gratefully left his office. Unfortunately, Robert failed to document this incident as well as his warning about what would happen if future infractions were to occur. He also failed to report this to the personnel office.

But he hadn't found out why the man had been cheating on his expense accounts. Was he fundamentally a crook? Or had there been some compelling financial need? If Miller's motivation was need, how was the problem going to be solved in the future apart from stealing?

Three weeks later his father came storming into his office. "You should have dumped that guy Miller!"

"Why?" Robert said. "I'm watching him more closely now; he's doing fine."

"First," his father shouted, his blood pressure rising to make his face red, "you're the president of this company, not the honesty watchdog, and we can't afford to hire a detective. But do you know how I heard about this mess?"

Robert shook his head.

"Stewart told me. Seems he overheard Nelson and some other sales reps talking. They're livid! They work their tails off while you coddle this freeloader. It was Nelson who originally won that account seven years ago! I warned you, Robert." The senior Wilford shook his finger in Robert's face. "You thought you were playing social worker, being Mr. Nice Guy, but it doesn't work that way! You've demoralized your best honest workers. I told you, you need to be tough! It's best for everyone." And his father stomped out before he had another heart attack.

The new president was an emotional wreck for the next week. What his father had said had a ring of truth, but it was so contrary to Robert's nature. *What if that act of leniency had been the very thing to turn Miller's life around?* Robert thought. *Isn't that worth something? And why should I feel ashamed of giving one of my employees a second chance? I would have done the same for any of them.* Then, the moment he thought it, he realized his actions weren't a brief lapse of judgment, but that he was fundamentally a different person from his father. If his father's way was the right way to run this company, then maybe he wasn't the man to follow in his footsteps. But . . . what could he do about it now?

Robert was experiencing tension typical of individuals who are gifted with helping talents but hold supervisory positions. The natural inclination is to reach out and help, not hurt. Robert's need to be tough-minded was in direct opposition to his helping and multi-relational, people-pleasing nature.

That week, while Robert was dictating a letter, Greg Franks, the vice president of finance, popped his head in to Robert's office. "Oh. I don't mean to bother you, Robert. I have these contracts ready for you to review, but I can see you're kind of preoccupied right now, so I'll just send you a memo on them. Okay?"

"Oh, fine, Greg. Just keep me posted." Robert said . . . not realizing the implications of what had just happened. Until that point, Greg had talked over all contract decisions with Robert. It was the policy Robert's father had set up to monitor Greg's weak sense of judgment. Now he was going to merely "report" the decision, after the fact. But since everything seemed to be going fine, Robert—still trying to juggle all the demands of being president—let it go.

But in doing so, Greg had assumed significant new authority by reducing his accountability to Robert. This arrangement continued until Greg made a major error in a contract that lost Wilford Electronics a large amount of money and a very important customer. It was a simple misunderstanding in an order, something Robert probably would have caught if he had been more involved. Not only was the invoice incorrect, but Greg's attempt to patch up his error was so poor that the order was canceled.

Robert called his father. "I'm really sorry, Dad. I just wasn't watching things as closely as I should. Do you think you could get that customer back if you got on the phone right away? I've tried, and no luck."

The older Wilford spoke tersely. "I should have fired Greg before you took over," he groused. "He means well, but he always tries to do things on his own. He fancies himself as an independent operator, but he doesn't have the skills for it. That's why I told you to watch him! Let this be a lesson to you. But this time I'm not going to bail you out; get that customer back by yourself. Maybe you'll guard your customers more closely in the future." The phone line went dead.

That night when he went home Robert realized the stress at the office just didn't leave him any energy to respond to the family. He flipped on the TV and stared at the screen, not even knowing what he was watching.

"Robert, I asked whether we could host the neighborhood Christmas-caroling party this year. I think it's our turn," Beth said from the family-room doorway.

Robert wasn't even sure how long she had been standing there. *This is no time to take on something extra*, he thought. But he rallied himself to answer, "Yeah, go ahead, Dear, but I can't promise to do much." He wanted to say, "I don't know if I'll even be around, come Christmas."

Back at the office the next morning, Robert recommitted himself to making things work. He just needed to dig in a little harder, he thought, and it would all come around. But when one of the sales reps dropped in while he was reading a report, Robert invited him in to talk. *I've always had an open-door policy*, he reasoned to himself. *After all, people are the backbone of this company. I can read reports anytime.* He spent half the morning talking to the rep, though the man offered to leave at least twice. But that afternoon, when he needed to make a decision based on the report, Robert still had not read it.

In reality, Robert was starting to come apart.

Somewhere during the next few weeks he picked up an article about midlife crises. That must be it. I'm having a midlife crisis, he muttered to himself. Everything has lost its luster. I need something new.

His father saw his distraction, too, and offered some advice: "You ought to go to some business seminars or take a management course. Here, read this book on management. It'll get you going again. Everybody has a slump from time to time."

Robert resented his father telling him what to do. *I'm no longer a kid*, he thought. *If I'm going to be the president, I'm going to have to assert my authority, even over him.* His wife and even some other loyal friends at the company had previously encouraged him to do that. But right now he realized he had made serious mistakes with the company precisely because he had not followed his father's advice. This was no time to resist his father . . . and that galled him.

In a very tense meeting a few days later, Robert told his father that he intended to reorganize the company and planned to hire a consultant to help him do so. His father, whose health had improved, didn't like the idea but agreed to go along with it. Robert was using outside assistance to compensate for his inherent lack of supervisory talent.

Robert hired an organizational consultant he really liked, and before long began relying heavily on his counsel. It felt good to achieve more autonomy from his father. But he pushed down the nagging thought that it did not represent real independence but was rather a transfer of dependence. Unfortunately, the consultant's ethics were questionable. He began to see Robert as a gravy train and began making himself indispensable to Wilford's corporate picture. Lacking discernment, Robert trusted him without instituting a system of checks and balances.

Together, Robert and the consultant decentralized control of the company so Robert became more of a facilitator than a controller. Robert's father disapproved when he began to see this happening, but with the consultant, Robert felt he had the support to go against his father.

Robert tried to keep a closer eye on the contractual decisions Greg made as vice president of finance, but Greg had developed a new system of accounting and reporting that Robert did not understand. It looked beautiful on paper, and Greg kept saying it was the newest method, but the result was that Robert became totally dependent on the vice president to interpret where the company stood.

A year later, the director of manufacturing requested approval to make major investments in new equipment. "We can get a tremendous price as an introductory deal," urged the division head. "The old machines aren't going to last much longer, and this could be our best opportunity." But Robert was under Greg's thumb in terms of understanding the corporate finances and dependent on his consultant in matters of management. The consultant urged Robert to trust Greg; Greg, always fiscally conservative, did not want to spend the money to upgrade the machinery. Robert turned down the proposal.

Within six months, the old equipment began to break down. Parts for the old machines were hard to find, and a major section of the plant was idle for two days. They would no sooner get one machine repaired when another one would break down. Finally, Robert went to see the director of manufacturing: "Let's go ahead and get the new equipment," he directed.

"I'm sorry, sir," the man responded. "It's going to cost us a lot more now, plus there could be a six-week wait before it is delivered."

It's my fault, Robert chided himself as he walked back to his office, and I'm not going to make anyone else pay. Though he realized the vice president of finance had given bad advice, Robert didn't want to reclaim the authority Greg had assumed or make Greg take the rap for a bad decision—it would seem like he was just trying to blame someone else. So he just braced himself for his father's wrath.

That evening Beth noted, "Robert, you were so happy in the earlier days of your job. Now, as president of the company, it seems like every day you are wringing your hands over some big crisis. Don't you think there's something more to life than trying to act like your father and showing him that you can do it? I believe you're a very gifted man, but your role as president of the company isn't allowing you to be your very best."

Robert didn't have much time to think about what Beth had said, because the next day the director of manufacturing delivered his resignation. "I'm sorry, sir," he said, when Robert asked why, "but I just don't think Wilford Electronics is doing very well, and I'm at the age that I can't afford to pass up a more secure offer."

Robert didn't miss the significance of that last comment. It not only stung but frightened him . . . especially when the director of manufacturing was the first of half a dozen middle management people to jump ship in the next few months. Robert tried to calm the concerns of the remaining personnel by promoting from within with very little consideration of qualifications. His consultant approved. "We've got to stop the bloodletting," he said. "We can afford to lose the dissatisfied people; dissatisfied workers are not good workers, anyway. Internal promotions will demonstrate your loyalty to those who are loyal to you."

Business stabilized for about three months. Then the army rejected a major shipment of Wilford products because of "poor workmanship" and initiated an investigation, threatening a major lawsuit. Robert was devastated. Not only had the army become such a major customer that Wilford would not be able to survive without government contracts, but they could not afford a lawsuit.

The next day Robert got a telephone call from a group of investors asking whether he wanted to sell the company. "What made you think it was for sale?" he snapped.

It turned out that his old director of manufacturing had organized the group of investors. Apparently, the group had not known about the problems with the army contract, but they thought Wilford might be interested in a change.

"We'd be glad to maintain you on a transitional basis for at least a year," the voice on the other end of the line assured Robert, "but we would insist on restructuring the top management."

Robert slammed down the phone. It seemed like he had no choice but to sell, but he could not face the prospect of telling his father they might lose the company. Robert called in his consultant, but the man shrugged. He gave a few explanations but refused to accept any responsibility for the problem.

In desperation, Robert finally went to his minister, confessing his pride and stubbornness and asking for help. "I always thought I was a leader," Robert acknowledged. "That's the role everyone put me in. I always seemed able to do it, but in six short years I've driven this company into the ground. I guess I'm not the leader I always thought I was."

"Well, that could be; that could be," agreed his minister thoughtfully. "But maybe there's more than one kind of leader. There's no question that you did have something going for you all those years when so many people put their trust in you. What was it you were actually doing when things went well?"

We've now come to the pinnacle of Robert's pursuit of leadership. He had a jump start into the fast lane because of his high school and college popularity. His winsome nature allowed him to network with a wide variety of people who admired him and considered him successful.

Under the umbrella of his father, Robert had made some assumptions. First of all, he presumed that the stability and respect for the presidency came with the office. He quickly learned that respect for the position came only if merited by the character of the person holding the office. It took only a few tough decisions to reveal his true ability to handle that position. Robert also learned that some subordinates (including good ones) were constantly seeking ways to acquire more authority. Once these individuals began to get the notion that they could get on the boss's good side, it was just a matter of time until he felt trapped by his position.

Robert's father, in his zeal to promote his son, had also made a typical family-business error: attempting to attribute to his son certain inherent qualities that he possessed but Robert did not. His assumption was that Robert could learn to behave like a supervisor when, in fact, his talents were not suited to that role.

Robert's problem is a common one. His first mistaken assumption was that helping talents are compatible with the demands of supervisory responsibilities. Rather, helping talents are generally reactive: They seek to affirm and encourage individuals one by one. Supervisory talents (Managing, Initiating, and Planning), on the other hand, are proactive. They deal with the large picture. They do not slow down for the needs of individuals and in some cases can be seen as insensitive.

In addition to Robert's helping talents, his winsome nature (i.e., his MultiRelational talent) put him at a second disadvantage as the senior executive. His pattern of constantly pleasing people developed a habit of never evaluating or properly judging people's performance. As a typical multirelational person, Robert would always look on the good side of a person and reject any negative information. When he accepted the role as CEO, he did not shift gears to become more critical of others' strengths and weaknesses.

The irony is that Robert truly has the capacity to be an effective leader. Unfortunately, through decisions of his own, yet also through the guidance of others, he chose the wrong leadership ladder. With this spiraling failure, it is not surprising that Robert will hit bottom, become depressed, and have no clue how to work his way out of his dilemma.

His one confidant—the consultant to whom he has entrusted himself—has left him. His wife, whom he feels he has betrayed, continues to support him, but he feels helpless. All of the things that have worked for him in his life have now come to a standstill. We can truly say that Robert is experiencing a midlife crisis. In the next phase, we will begin to see how Robert slowly pulls himself out of this predicament.

The good news is that Robert still is gifted. For the very reasons that he was voted "Most Likely to Succeed" and was popular in high school, he still has great potential. The critical need here is for Robert to find the right ladder to climb.

Chapter

New Roles

Diana Slater Barber

Diana did not know why Jim had asked for a special time to talk with her. Why did he need an appointment when they talked every day? It made her uneasy.

They had walked three blocks with awkward silences and insignificant chatter about the kids' home-schooling lessons when Jim finally said, "I don't want you to receive this as a criticism, so I waited until we could talk without any other distractions. . . . "

Diana waited, then finally urged, "So? Go ahead." But she wasn't sure she really wanted him to continue.

"Well, in the last few weeks you have been exceptionally irritable, and I just wondered if something was bothering you."

"Jim, I can't respond to such sweeping generalizations. What are you talking about? Give me some specifics."

"Okay, for the last three evenings . . . " and he described how she had lost her temper with the kids. He also reminded her of a couple fights they had had recently and one she had gotten into with her best friend. "None of that's like you, Diana. You are too good for these kinds of outbursts."

If she had been irrational before, nothing could have intensified the stress more than these accusations! But she tried to control herself and, finally, she had to admit that Jim was right. She had felt it, too . . . a certain mounting pressure, the feeling that a steel spring within her was wound too tight.

"I'll try to relax, take life a little easier," she promised.

But a month later Jim brought up the problem again. "I think you ought to go to the doctor," he said. "Maybe there's some kind of physiological imbalance that you could easily correct. It's not going to work to tighten the screws down on yourself. Something else is going on."

Diana made an appointment with the doctor. Physically, everything was okay, the doctor told her, but he recommended she see a therapist for some counseling. Diana was shocked. All her life she was the one who had it all together. She was the stable one on whom others leaned. The doctor explained that her prominent role in the community made it important that she work out anything that was bothering her.

Reluctantly, Diana selected a woman psychologist who also happened to share her religious values. At the first session, Diana fussed and fumbled somewhat apologetically while trying to explain why she had come. But the counselor was very perceptive and was soon asking Diana about her experience in various committees and church business meetings. Diana couldn't see the relevance of the discussion until late in the second session when the counselor explained that she had had experiences very similar to Diana's.

"I went through many of the same patterns you describe," the woman explained. "In high school, in dating men, and at college I was always out there organizing things. When that wasn't possible—for whatever reason—I withdrew. If I couldn't physically withdraw from the situation, I became miserable. This became most evident in my first professional job, right after I passed my state licensing boards. I worked in a clinic that was highly structured but poorly managed. I couldn't stand it. In fact, before long I began exhibiting some very disturbing symptoms. If I had stayed on, they might have locked me up. I was throwing fits and blowing up at my best friends, including my husband. And then I had the opportunity to open this practice for myself, and I've loved it ever since."

The woman smiled at Diana. "It could be that you are naturally gifted with the ability to supervise others, like me. If so, we are people who naturally take charge and are uncomfortable when we cannot. It is the same in men or women. Unfortunately, women are not accepted in that role as easily as men. Think about that idea this next week."

Diana went home very troubled. "I just don't understand," she said to Jim. "I always thought that I was to be a wife who would be happy supporting her pastor husband, but the more I think about what my counselor said, the more I get the feeling that she's right. A behind-the-scenes person is not what I'm meant to be."

"But you're very good at supporting me," Jim said. "You always give me good advice about church politics. I've come to rely on you. Why would you want to be anything else but a pastor's wife? We've both agreed that God called us to the ministry. This is just a time of testing. You can't let doubts creep in."

"I'm not saying that I want to quit, Jim. I'm just saying that I need some kind of adjustment. My counselor was right. All my life I've taken charge. It feels natural to me, and when I can't, I'm very frustrated. I can't let that frustration continue indefinitely over months and years or it may lead to bitterness."

"But you do take charge of our home . . . and the kids . . . and a lot of things!"

"I know, and for a long time that seemed satisfying. But I have mastered that. It's like I have this desire to reach higher levels of proficiency in my taking charge of things."

Jim frowned. "You sound like you're power hungry."

Diana realized that the conversation was deteriorating and they were both feeling threatened, so she brought it to an end. But she kept thinking about what her counselor had said. In some significant way now that she was forty, she did not fit the mold she had fashioned for herself.

Her mother had been the supportive homemaker type, but Diana was more like her father, who managed the lumberyard in Waterston. She began to realize that though Jim seemed like her father because of his commanding presence in front of people and his speaking ability, he did not manage people like her father did. *Can it be*, wondered Diana, *that someone can be a great preacher and a poor manager of people?* The more she thought about it, the more certain she was. She was always guiding Jim when it came to issues related to managing people.

The next time Diana met with her counselor, she revealed some fears she had about discovering who she was. "I don't know that I want to be a take-charge kind of woman," she said. "I've always despised bossy women."

"Who says you have to be bossy to exercise your talent for supervising others?" the counselor asked.

"Well, no one, but that's the image I have, some kind of a Captain Bly in a skirt."

The counselor laughed. "There is a degree of taking charge that comes with the aptitude for supervising others, and since some people naturally dislike anyone telling them what to do, a certain degree of complaints comes with the territory. But you need to realize that managers must be concerned with the big picture, and they don't always stop to smell the roses and talk to the workers along the way. That's what the people with helping talents do. But to be a good manager, you don't have to be heavy-handed."

During the weeks while Diana was meeting with her therapist, Jim felt that the most loving thing to do was spare her all the tensions of church politics. So he did not tell her how Bob Fraser, the chairman of the board, was taking over more and more of the building program. But one day the tension came to a head again. "Jim," said Fraser when they were alone, "I hate to cross you again, like I had to with the financing of this new building, but I know what I'm doing here. We need to go with the R-39 insulation."

"But that seems excessive for this region. No government publication recommends it. It'll just be a waste."

"I've already ordered it."

"You can't do that," snapped Jim.

"I can, and I have," Fraser said firmly. "Listen, Jim, it's time we get one thing straight. I'm the chairman of the board. The board hired you to minister to us spiritually. You pay attention to that, and let me handle the rest of the details around here. Either do that, or things could get rough for you."

Jim was stunned. He motioned weakly toward the door, and Bob Fraser had the grace to leave without saying more, but once he was out, Jim fell apart. It seemed like all he thought he was—his stature, his credibility, his role as a leader—had just been taken away. He was devastated.

At home during the days that followed, Jim couldn't bring himself to share with Diana what had happened at church and slowly sank into a depression. When she finally got the story out of him, she marched into the kitchen and picked up the phone before he could stop her. "Bob Fraser, please," she said into the receiver. When Fraser answered, she confronted him for making a power play on her husband, for not being spiritually submissive to his pastor.

When she had finished, Fraser said, "Diana, you're out of line. This is none of your business. I'm sorry, I've got to go now, but don't worry. We'll work it out."

Diana was incensed, but it also deeply embarrassed her that Jim was such a weakling. Why couldn't he stand up for himself?

The next day, her husband was so depressed that he did not go into the office. He stayed home the following day as well. When Diana asked if he was sick, all he would say was, "No, I'm not sure I'm fit to lead our church. I need time to think things over."

Three times the next day Fraser tried to phone him, but Jim wouldn't return his calls. "You can't just ignore the man," said Diana. "Now's the time to get in there and reclaim your authority." But Jim wouldn't respond.

Thursday Jim called the associate pastor and, without giving explanation, asked him to preach on Sunday. Late the following Tuesday night, there was a knock on the door. Diana answered it to find Bob Fraser standing on the step. "I need to talk to Jim," he said.

When Jim came out in his bathrobe, Fraser got right to the point. "We had a board meeting tonight," he said. "We cannot continue this way. We are giving you a three-month leave of absence. The associate pastor will fill in, and we recommend that you get some rest. After two months, we'd like you to meet with us to discuss the future. Maybe we can work things out then, but we just cannot go on this way."

Diana wanted to be supportive of and comforting to her husband, but she was overwhelmed with an inexpressible loathing for his inability to stand up to Fraser. "Why didn't you do something?" Her tone was very intense; it peaked at the level of a drill sergeant's: "Get with the program." This involuntary impulse, totally out of character, surprised her and caused Jim to wince. Yet, true to form, the real Diana, with her take-charge drive, was coming out. Rather than comforting her husband in retreat, she was taking the offensive.

All Jim could mumble back was, "Do what? What could I do?"

In the days that followed, Jim sank into deeper depression. He would go into long periods of silence, refusing to eat or get out of bed. Diana's psychologist recommended that to help him, she back off. "Jim will have to face this himself," she said. "Encourage him, yet don't do it for him."

"Promise me one thing," Diana said to Jim. "I want you to see a counselor who works with pastors. He was recommended by my psychologist."

"You think I'm going crazy?"

"No, that's not it. I've been seeing a psychologist, and I'm not crazy. But I believe these problems have a lot to do with who we are and what we've been trying to do with our lives. She tells me that when our talents and our occupation don't match, no one can sustain the tension forever. The person either dies inside or blows up. For us, it looks like I'm blowing up while you, you're regressing."

Reluctantly, Jim went to the counselor. During the sessions, he discovered that he always had loved studying and preaching. It was trying to manage people that created problems for him. "I guess I never liked business meetings or conflict or telling people what to do, but I used to be able to do it. Lately, however, it's felt so tedious. I end up pulling away from conflict. How come I can't manage anymore? I used to be good at it."

"Maybe you don't have a talent for managing people. If that's the case, you were always reaching beyond yourself to do what managing you did. Now, at age forty-one, you don't have as much energy as you had when you were younger, and it's harder," he said.

"Younger? I'm not that old! I should be hitting my career prime, and now everything is blowing up."

"You aren't old, but you are older than you used to be, so you can't press forward on raw grit. Besides, you have many more demands on your energy now . . . a wife who is expressing her own needs, teenagers at home, and I bet your parents are starting to need more attention now, too."

The conversations continued with the counselor suggesting that Jim was in a textbook career crunch. He had succeeded in his early years by applying his overall drive and winsome nature. But now he just didn't have the energy to keep up the demands of a job that didn't match his talents. The counselor pointed out that Jim's predicament was a very common one among ministers and those in supervisory roles in other helping professions.

"How would you feel if you had a position where you spent most of your time studying and preaching and you weren't expected to manage a church?" the counselor asked.

"That would be great," Jim responded. "But who's going to pay me for that?"

"It's been arranged before," he said. "It's not the norm, but some churches with the right staff have put it together. If it doesn't work out with your church, you might become a traveling evangelist or a public-relations speaker for a Christian college or university."

That night, for the first time in weeks, Jim began to feel a deep glow inside. Maybe he was okay just as he was. He could make a contribution with his life.

He cautiously shared his feelings with Diana.

"It sounds like a hopeful direction," Diana said. "Would you like me to go with you when you present this to the board?"

Diana went with Jim to talk with the board. She was determined to avoid trying to manage the meeting, but she needed to know all the nuances of what happened.

Once Jim had outlined the possibility of becoming a speaking pastor rather than a managing pastor, Bob Fraser responded, "It's funny you should mention that, because that has been on my mind for some time. We like the way you preach, Jim. That's what drew us to you in the first place. I really think this is worth serious consideration."

"But that doesn't satisfy the other pastoral needs in this church," said one of the other board members.

"That's true," said Jim. "But I've been thinking about that, too. Our associate pastor is really best in ministering to people. He can fill in at the pulpit once in a while, but he's not really a preacher..."

"I've been noticing that," interrupted another board member. Everyone chuckled nervously.

"And maybe," said Jim, rather tentatively, "maybe it would be best if the board considered hiring an executive pastor to run the operation here."

Diana almost choked on hearing those words because they went so strongly against the image of a pastor with which she had grown up. But for her husband's sake, she kept quiet and listened.

"It might work," said a board member who had been in the navy. "But it feels kind of precarious. Usually the captain of the ship is the one in charge."

"That's true for the navy," said Coleman, a retired businessman of a large retail chain, "but navy commanders don't have to be speakers. It won't be easy, but if we find the right executive pastor who can form a bond with Jim, I think it could work. I'm for giving it a try. Just one question, Jim," he said shifting his attention. "Are you willing to give up the status of being the head honcho? Whoever we hire will want a piece of the action."

"I think so," said Jim.

"Well, I also think it's a good idea," said Bob Fraser.

Diana cringed. Bob was a good man, and she trusted that he loved God, but she also could see that he was a strong-minded, take-charge person—perhaps somewhat like herself. Because, the truth of the matter was, there was no one else on the board who really challenged Bob for that role. Over the years, he had eliminated the opposition. She felt a twinge of fear; then the old adage, "It takes one to know one," crossed her mind, and she smiled to herself. *That's true*, she thought. *If Bob and I were on the same team, one of us would have to step aside because there's not room for two managers. But maybe if the other players aren't trying to manage, he'll do a great job.*

As they left the meeting, Diana promised herself not to use Jim as an avenue to challenge Bob Fraser for control of the church. Her counselor had told her, "You have to have your own turf. You can't be borrowing somebody else's." But, if supervising others was a strength God had given her, who was she going to supervise?

In this chapter, we see two critical issues. First, we see what happens when a person underevaluates his or her aptitudes and tries to fit an unsuitable role. Diana was attempting to be something that didn't fit her. Her values overrode the direct application of her natural talents. She thought that she could fill the role of a reactive person when it appears that she is naturally more proactive.

In her earlier years Diana had sufficient energy to suppress the frustration of this reactive role; but now, in phase three, she is not only irritated but does not have the energy to control her impatience. Her talents are demanding to be used.

People don't always respond to stress and irritation by losing their tempers. Some retreat into depression. In Diana's case, if she had not wisely submitted to professional counsel, she could have destroyed her marriage and other relationships important to her. This would have further complicated the issue since the very role she was trying to protect—being a supportive wife—would, in fact, be damaged because of this compulsion to take charge.

I want to emphasize that one of the talents for supervising others is not a license to be domineering or manipulative. The traits of assertiveness, dominance, and manipulation are personality issues. Any one of the three talents for supervising others is more a predisposition to coordinate the activities of others. Both men and women have these talents. These talents are so strong that when a person who has them enters a room, the first thought is *Who's in charge and does that person know what he is doing? If not, I either must leave the room or take control.*

Diana now is facing the need to make a change. She wisely understands this and is willing to take the responsibility to move ahead. Unfortunately, too often in this phase, people are afraid or continue with business as usual. If that's the case, they begin to incur some severe emotional and medical problems. Not only do their relationships with others suffer, but so does their job performance.

In employment-interview situations, managers can be much more analytical when they interview persons who are in their forties, especially those who claim to have been let go due to "corporate cutbacks" or "reorganization." Managers know the trauma of having to let people go who once were good producers but now, because they are poorly suited to their jobs, have outlived their usefulness. So, when a manager has to interview a person of, say, forty, it is crucial to avoid inheriting someone else's problem.

Change at this point in a person's life is very hard, but the consequences are worse. Usually there are two options. The most common is to go back to school. This will be Diana's preferred choice. Going back to school is the least painful, the most honorable, and, unfortunately, the most expensive. But for the person who is the main provider for a family, further schooling is often financially impossible.

A second option is to secure the services of a professional mid-career consultant. Usually, within a period of six months, a person can expect to have identified his natural bent, have focused on a realistic career target, and be close to being employed in a new field without further training or education. Of course, there are no guarantees of prompt reemployment, but an effective career-transition consultant can help.

For someone to take the first job that comes along if it does not use one's talent strengths is almost worse than remaining depressed. When a person takes on an occupation that is below his capacity, he is essentially saying, "I have nothing to contribute." He has begun to design his coffin. He has turned off that little light inside that says "There is something that I can contribute. I want to make a difference." It impacts all of his thoughts, his relationships, his self-esteem. He begins to look for cheap substitutes to soothe the pain—substitutes such as alcohol or drugs or fast living, anything to help him forget.

In some cases such a person may try to showcase symbols of success by buying a new car, taking an extravagant vacation, or making other flamboyant acquisitions. If you are a person who needs to make a career change, I strongly encourage you to make the move now (with counsel) rather than gutting it out until retirement. I have counseled many people who have grown up in a home where the father lived just to retire. Even though they love their father, adult children will say, "One thing I know I don't want to do is live the painful life of my father."

Diana's husband gives us a couple of additional insights into this phase. His profile is similar to Robert's in the previous chapter. One difference, however, is that he chose to pursue his occupation, whereas Robert inherited his role.

Another difference is that Jim knew his strengths: Speaking, Ordering his time, and Researching. Yet, even though he knew these strengths, he made a common mistake. He had assumed that by looking good in front of others, he could also manage others, a misunderstanding common among people involved in ministry. Jim was a very organized person in his own personal effects, but that didn't mean he had the ability to manage people. Similarly, Jim was very effective in commanding respect in front of others, but that didn't translate into the ability to guide and direct and coordinate the activities of others. Any time someone is in charge, he will always be challenged on the decisions he makes. There is an old saying: "If the heat is too hot, get out of the kitchen." Since Jim chose to be a cook in the kitchen, he could not complain about people who were challenging him in those duties.

A second insight into Jim's situation is that he was dreaming of an ideal where he could be a preacher or speaker without the duties and responsibilities of management. In today's church, that is not a common role. Usually the person who preaches Sunday morning is the one who is expected to command and oversee the church the rest of the week. For churches of fewer than one hundred people, the congregation is not large enough to require the pastor to have a talent for supervision of others. If a person is a good speaker, however, it is only a matter of time until that speaking ability attracts new members. With a growing congregation, that pastor has an option to either spin out a daughter church or hire someone to help manage the congregation.

There is no question that bringing someone in to share the control and authority of the church requires humility. Very few people are able to share the responsibility. So, it's really up to Jim. If he wants to preach in a church where the general norm is for the preacher to be in charge, he will need to find someone that he can work with to help him share the responsibility of managing.

Negotiating one's job description is my first recommendation before quitting. Once a person finds that his or her talent strengths do not fit the job (and yet some are affirmed), then I highly recommend beginning to discuss with one's superior some way that an alternative path can be worked out.

Here's the key insight: The responsibility to come up with an alternate plan should not be placed on the senior executive or board. If you want to stay, then it is up to you to come up with a realistic option and make it work. It is also your responsibility to accept a trial period for approving the change. Any time you go against the norm, you need to take the responsibility to come up with the alternatives.

Many times I have helped clients negotiate alternate routes to strengthen and maintain their career paths, particularly in churches and corporations with higher-level executive or managerial positions. This is truly a fulfilling experience. Nevertheless, I need to underscore that it is delicate and does not automatically succeed.

As we turn to phase four for both Diana and Jim, we can eagerly anticipate how their decisions to change turn out.

Chapter 14

Recovery

Phil Grady

Three months after his accident, Phil still was not walking. One day, his physical therapist said, "You're not trying, Phil. You gotta push it. You gotta work at home. 'No pain, no gain,' you know."

"I'm doing my best. It's just . . . "

"Just what? Is it that you don't really want to walk again?"

"Of course I want to walk! Why wouldn't I?"

"Because maybe that truck didn't fall on you by accident."

"What? You think someone pushed it?"

"No, I mean that because of the stress on your job that you were unwilling to face and change, you took the easy way out and allowed an accident to happen. Maybe you subconsciously got careless. If it wasn't this, it could have been something else—a way to get out."

"You're crazy, man! Maybe you don't know how much pain I've been in. Why would I do a dumb thing like that?"

"I've seen it happen before, but it's just a hunch. I've been at this for over twenty-five years, and I keep learning all the time. Occasionally someone is after insurance money, but most of the time the person doesn't even realize what they've done."

"I thought you were a physical therapist, not a shrink. You don't know what you're talking about."

"I'm no shrink, but I keep my eyes open. Accidents happen, but when a person is not eager to recover and get back to work, it says something. What's it say in your case?"

"This is really nuts," said Phil. "Only a psycho would injure himself. What other reason could there be?"

The therapist shrugged. "There are a lot of reasons. Some people are addicted to the sympathy and attention they get when they've been hurt. They're the kind who are always hurting themselves . . . but not usually as badly as you've done. Sometimes, though, an injury is the only way a person can get out of an intolerable situation . . . like maybe a job or a marriage?"

"My marriage was fine until my wife left me," Phil said bitterly. "But that happened after the accident. She couldn't put up with all the pressure. Look, my time is up for today. Can I get out of here?"

"Sure. See you Friday."

The therapist hadn't actually suggested that Phil might have subconsciously been trying to get out of his job, and Phil didn't consider that possibility as he thought about the conversation later. But the idea that people might think he didn't want to get well made him mad; he determined to make more progress.

In the next few weeks, he showed remarkable improvement until he was walking short distances with only a cane for support. But his progress hit a plateau . . . just short of the mobility that would have allowed him to take the dispatcher's job at the fire station.

"When will you be back?" the chief asked one day when Phil stopped by to see how everyone was doing. It was ten months after the accident.

"Pretty soon, pretty soon. I'm getting around better all the time." But the truth was that three months had passed with no appreciable improvement.

"Say, something came in the mail the other day that I thought might interest you." The chief went into the office and shuffled through his stack of mail. "Ah, here it is. My wife's brother is a training-film producer in Los Angeles. They need a consultant who is an experienced firefighter. It might be something for you to do while you're recovering."

Phil took the envelope. "Thanks, Chief," he grinned wryly. "I always wanted to be in the movies. Maybe I could play the part after the stunt man falls off the ladder."

They both laughed.

But that afternoon at home, he forgot about the envelope because he was served papers by a sheriff's deputy: His wife was divorcing him. As he stared at the form, he couldn't believe it. He thought that after time Jennifer would surely come back.

The trauma of that news consumed him. It was a phone call from the fire chief a week later that reminded him of the envelope on his dresser. Only then did he open it and read the proposal for developing fire-safety training films that the Los Angeles company planned to produce. What they needed was an experienced fire-fighter to act as their consultant.

As Phil thought about the creative potential of working with a film company, the cloud that had been hanging over him when he thought of sitting at a desk filing reports lifted. He began to day-dream about the job while taking showers and during his therapy sessions.

The film studio was not the big Hollywood lot he had imagined, lined with cameras, costumes, and actors. It was just a drab three-story office building on a quiet street with poor excuses for palm trees. "Oh, we do most of our shooting on site," explained the receptionist when Phil asked. "If we need a studio set, we rent one for a few days."

The company had already made a series of films for coal-mine safety. Phil's first assignment was to watch those films. Within ten minutes, Phil was in love with the idea of making films. The possibility that his experience as a fireman might qualify him for such creative work was almost too much to imagine.

At the end of the afternoon, he went back to his motel and called his chief. "I know this is what I want to do," he explained. "I realize that it may delay my return to the station, but if there is any way you can you help me, I'd sure appreciate it."

The chief, a wise manager, chuckled. "I'll take care of things on this end. How long do they want you?"

"This project may last two or three months at most; that's what they tell me."

Phil went immediately to Los Angeles. Apparently, Phil learned later, he had impressed the producer by his enthusiasm for film-making after interviewing several other firefighters who wanted a job but had no real interest in the creative side of the project.

Two months later, Phil was walking with no more than a minor limp. His interest in the job absorbed most of his attention . . . but he was not so preoccupied that he didn't notice the nurse at the hospital where he went for his physical therapy. Her name tag read "Angela Lopez."

One day he realized that Angela was getting off duty just as he finished his whirlpool treatment. "Can I give you a lift home?" he asked hopefully. "We could stop for lunch somewhere." To his surprise, she agreed. Their hamburgers had just arrived when Angela asked Phil about his background. Suddenly, it seemed so remote and foreign to him. Memories of his parents' home, the military, and his old fire-station job made his stomach tighten so that he almost lost his appetite. Was I really that much out of my element, he wondered to himself, that I can't think about those settings without having a physical reaction?

But that did seem to be the case, because in a few minutes when Angela asked him what he was doing now, Phil had no trouble talking and eating. "Tomorrow we're going to shoot a sequence to demonstrate ventilating a building fire. I want to get that camera right inside the burning building, looking up through the smoke as a fireman chops a hole through the roof," Phil said as he stuffed the rest of his hamburger in his mouth.

Angela, it turned out, had been married before and had two children: José was in the fifth grade and Miguel was in third. She said she also attended church regularly. "It's one of the few things I can do to help keep them off drugs, especially since they don't have a father around."

Phil didn't miss the comment and its possible implication. A month later, when they'd enjoyed several dates, he reminded her of it and asked, "Did you mean that you might be interested in finding your boys a father sometime?"

"Well, if I found the right one," she said with a smile. "But I couldn't guarantee that they would accept him."

Somehow Phil managed to extend his consulting contract with the chief's approval. Within five months, Phil and Angela were married, but Angela was right: The kids did not accept him as their father. "You're not my dad," José challenged, "so you can't tell me what to do." Miguel picked up the same track and accentuated it with the upward jerk of his head.

Becoming an instant father was a very rocky time for Phil until he began coaching the park soccer team. Then, somehow, the boys quit testing him. They seemed proud that their stepfather was the coach.

The training film won a national award, and because of Phil's success in consulting on the film, the company president called him in and said, "Phil, you're a natural. Why weren't you doing this before?" And then he asked Phil to stay on to advise on other training film projects.

Two years later, Phil was still on the job, having assisted with several films. The fire-safety film series was followed by several others—two winning more awards. The series was used by fire departments all across the country.

Phil knew the film industry was not as secure as his former job. There was no pension, no retirement benefits, and limited health insurance. But his wife had a job. And the value he had previously placed on security had been overridden by the explosive exuberance of using his natural talents. He had never won an award for anything before, and now as a virtual novice in filmmaking, he had three to his name.

In spite of Phil's job satisfaction, life wasn't perfect. The Gradys took a terrible loss on the house they bought. They were soon hiring contractors to install a new sewer system and roof, when they had thought all the house needed was a coat of paint. When they finally decided they couldn't afford the place, they discovered it had been overappraised and wouldn't sell for anything near what they had paid for it. If he had been in his old job, such a loss would have torn Phil apart. But his new enthusiasm for life overrode the financial strain.

Reluctantly, Phil and Angela stuck it out and in time made the house "home." It was often in disarray, but they kept it clean, and Angela didn't seem to mind Phil's clutter.

Phil found the congestion and smog of Los Angeles unpleasant and was sometimes homesick for the simplicity of Waterston. But it was not worth trading the inner peace he had found, so he looked for other ways to get away from the city. After a few years, he found a music group in which he could play his trumpet. He also bought a boat and went fishing whenever he could. Bobbing gently on a nearby lake with his line in the water, Phil thought that the boat just about rounded out his life. He wasn't wealthy, but if you had asked him, he would have told you that he didn't lack for anything he really needed. Maybe his parents would never understand, but oddly, he did understand. He was going to make a difference with his life.

Remember that C+ student who blended into the woodwork and never did anything outstanding? The boy who came from a good family and had a slight glaze over his eyes as he looked at life? Now, in phase three, he has somehow acquired a turbo charge.

I have seen this happen, not only in phase three but in phase four. Something clicks. That "click" is a person seeing that how they are put together, just the way they are, can fit into this world, and that by exercising their strengths they can make a difference. It is kind of a rippling feeling that goes through your body and produces goose bumps.

Phil Grady had experienced a lot of pain in his life prior to this time. He lost his wife and children, whom he deeply loved. More importantly, he did not understand the confusion caused by his incompatibility with his work world. He had inherited from his parents a value for security and stability that was affirmed by the military and the fire department. He had been trained to be highly structured, to maintain an established order of things. He had also been taught to disdain innovative, creative behavior; so everything that this new media production position represented was contrary to his upbringing.

It is one thing for a person to realize that his present position doesn't fit. It is another to find something better. It took me a long time as a counselor to realize that truth. In my early years, it wasn't that difficult to evaluate a person's strengths and current position and to remark, "It doesn't appear that you are suited for being a salesperson or a manager." But until I had something better to offer, the person would just shrug in discouragement and walk away.

As we look at new opportunities that may fit our aptitudes, as we research and evaluate them, we get closer to them. By that very act, we distance ourselves from the current position that we hold on to so tightly. Sometimes the change is facilitated by a well-meaning friend or boss. In this case, perhaps the fire chief was more perceptive than Phil realized. He knew that Phil had come to the end of his line and that the assignment to the desk was no reward for all his years of hard work. Perhaps he initiated the call to his sister or recalled some offhand comment of months earlier. In this chapter, the focus is not so much on how Phil got the new job. The focus is the tension between preserving this desire for stability, order, and security with the dramatic impact of performing in a new role.

The story is not over for Phil, however. Since this turnaround was something that he had not planned for nor understood, we will see that in phase four some unfortunate consequences will befall him. Nevertheless, it is important to note that Phil's new employer commented that he was "a natural." I have witnessed many situations where, within a few months, a person introduced into a new field fits naturally and, out of his own zeal, works overtime to get up to speed. In so doing, such a person can surpass those who have been working in the field for many years.

Chapter

Evidence of Excellence

Claire Winters Sorenson

C laire hadn't wanted a thirty-fifth-birthday party, so David decided to surprise her with something a little different. He arranged for four-year-old Kevin to sleep over with his best friend from nursery school. Then he somehow kept Claire from starting dinner, saying, "Not now. Let's wait a while," whenever she headed for the kitchen.

Finally, about seven-thirty, the doorbell rang. When Claire answered the door, she found a waiter and waitress dressed in formal black and white balancing huge linen-covered trays on their shoulders. They swept into the dining room and deposited the trays on the table, then returned to their van for other delectables.

"I've never heard of such a thing," marveled Claire as the servers scurried around.

Within minutes, Claire found herself sitting across the table from David in flickering candlelight with a beautiful meal spread out between them . . . and the caterers were gone.

"How will they get their stuff back?" Claire asked in amazement.

"They'll pick it up tomorrow morning . . . after ten," said David with a smile. "Don't forget, tomorrow's Saturday, and we can sleep in. Best of all, they'll do all the cleanup."

Later, as they were sipping coffee kept piping hot in a carafe, David said, "I've noticed that things seem to have been going a lot better between you and Kevin the last few months. Am I right?"

"Yeah, I guess that's true. Somehow I feel different about him . . . No. Come to think of it, I think it's myself I feel different about."

"What do you mean?"

"Ever since I started working for the *Community Marquee*, I feel like I've received a new lease on life. I finally feel like I'm going somewhere. It's not that it's so big, but . . . well, I guess I really want to thank you, because you believed in me when I didn't even believe in myself."

Later that year, the magazine began sending Claire to neighboring cities to review the better community theaters as they produced new plays. Claire developed a regular column that began to be quoted and used by the local theaters in their advertising.

Then one day when she was in Baltimore reviewing a play, a man asked if she would be interested in reviewing movies.

"But *Community Marquee* doesn't review movies," Claire protested.

"We know that. We weren't thinking of *Community Marquee*. We would syndicate your reviews to smaller newspapers all over the country. Who knows? Maybe someday you will become another Siskel and Ebert." The man grinned.

"All over the country? But how would I see all those new movies in time to write a timely review? I can't go to Hollywood all the time."

"That wouldn't be necessary. Usually the studios arrange regional advance showings for a new film. You'd only have to go to Hollywood occasionally for a really big release. We've even been trying to arrange video reviews for some films, but the studios are afraid of piracy."

"How many reviews would you want a week?"

"We'd begin with one per week, but that could increase."

Claire asked if she could have some time to consider the idea, but she knew she wanted the assignment. When she talked it over with David, he agreed that it was a great opportunity and urged her to go ahead.

Three months later, she had written twelve reviews and was receiving strong encouragement from the syndicate—they had sold her column to 137 newspapers, and from the responses, they were confident of expanding to many others. What surprised Claire most was that people most often mentioned the thoughtful, literary evaluations she included in her material.

Then one day she ran into Roger Maynard, one of the reporters she had known at the *Globe*.

"Well, if it isn't Claire Winters," he said with a tone that suggested he was surprised she was still alive. "How's it going?"

"Pretty well, Roger. What are you doing these days?"

"Oh, I'm an investigative reporter at the *Globe*. I cover all the hot stuff, you know: politics, crime, whatever takes some real digging."

"I'll have to watch more closely for your byline," Claire said. She still read the *Globe* regularly and had never noticed his name associated with a major article.

Roger did not miss the implication of her comment, and it shocked him that the reclusive, almost frightened Claire he had known years earlier had developed the ability to bite back. "You still writing for that little magazine—what's it about? Community theaters or something?"

"Yes, the *Community Marquee*. I'm still on staff, but I don't get to spend as much time with it as I used to."

"I would imagine it gets pretty boring working for a small specialty publication like that, doesn't it? I mean, your readers are pretty much a bunch of would-be actors, aren't they? But I suppose they like reading about themselves."

"They're a little more sophisticated than that. Some community theater is very high caliber. But, no, I don't get bored with the publication. I'm most interested in developing the quality of my writing."

"Well, good for you. You just keep working on it. And someday, if you feel like you have a really good feature or something, shoot me a copy. I'll be glad to look it over and see if we can't find a place for it in the *Globe*. Who knows? You might break into the real world of publishing some day," he grinned.

"I think I have enough of that right now." Claire returned the smile. "I have a column that is syndicated in 137 newspapers all across the country." She paused to let that sink in. "And the *Globe* is one of them. Hey, Roger, it's been good to see you. We should keep in touch. Here's my card," and she turned and left. She could have gone much farther to put him in his place, but why?

That evening she couldn't help laughing when she told David about her encounter. "You know, two years ago the implication of his comments—that I was not capable of professional work—would have crushed me. But lately I've come to realize that what others think of me is not nearly so important as what I think of myself. And I've come to believe that I am a gifted writer. I take great pleasure in that."

She snuggled closer to David. "I actually was sad that Roger needs to put someone else down to lift himself up. But I hope the next time he's tempted to do it, he'll hesitate before criticizing a colleague. The person may not have the self-confidence to take it. I sure wouldn't have had it a couple years ago."

When Claire turned forty, her son, Kevin, asked her what life was like when she was a kid. She described her school days as a young girl in Waterston, when she didn't have many friends and always felt awkward. She told about family picnics, Christmas at her grandparents' farm . . . and Sputnik. "It was the first artificial satellite ever launched into space. That was 1957, and I was a little younger than you are now, Kevin. The Russians did it, and the United States became worried that they were surpassing us in scientific achievements, so there was a big push to upgrade education. We had to study twice as hard."

She had just launched into the assassination of President Kennedy and civil rights marches when Kevin decided he'd heard enough and drifted off to watch television.

But later that evening David returned to the nostalgia theme as well. "If you had a chance to live your youth all over, would you do it any differently?"

Claire thought for some time and then said, "That's a hard question, because the things I'd change have to do with what I've learned in the last few years. I didn't know them when I was younger, so I didn't really have a choice."

"Well, then, knowing what you know now, what would you do differently?"

"First, I would relax with other people. I used to feel so out of it, like something was wrong with me because I didn't have a swirl of friends around me all the time. But I don't really like being with a lot of people, and I certainly am uncomfortable with strangers.

"Now I know that's okay," she went on. "I have only a few close friends and like it that way, but when I was a kid, I felt so awkward with other people that it was hard to relax and develop one or two close friendships."

Claire paused and stared off into space until David prodded, "Go on. What else would you change?"

"Kids used to tease me about being a brain. I was our high school valedictorian, graduated with a 4.0. I was actually embarrassed about it! Wish I could have come to appreciate my talents a lot earlier, then I would have had confidence in them and put them to use. I like to write, and now I'm finding that I can do it well. I like to do research and watch for details. I like everything in its right place. I'm an orderly person. All those things have their value, but I never knew that when I was younger. . . . Hey," she said. "Don't leave your mug on the coffee table. Put it in the dishwasher!"

That struck David's funny bone, and he kept teasing her until they'd gotten ready for bed and turned out the light.

Then in the darkness Claire said, "Oh. There's one other thing, David. I went on and got my Ph.D., but at the time it was a stalling technique to avoid entering the "real world." I did it mostly because school was a safe place. Beyond that, I didn't realize its value. Now I see that academic achievements can be helpful or harmful. They're not an end in themselves, but they are significant when they develop your innate talents. On the other hand, if one doesn't do well, it can hurt one's self-image. Looking back on it, I can see that my degrees could have been that for me and given me lots more confidence. But I didn't see it at the time. It wasn't until you started believing in me and I finally proved to myself what I could do, that I began to believe I had anything to contribute to this world. You know what I mean?"

But David didn't respond; he had already dozed off.

Although it has been more than twenty years since Claire left high school, in phase three the profound influence of the self-image formed during that time can still be seen. Unless a person has grown beyond those early self-perceptions, the memories of those years can be haunting ones.

Unfortunately, Claire has repeatedly misinterpreted her academic performance. She viewed it as an escape. She hid in the zeal of pursuing her studies and failed to recognize that in her noteworthy achievement she was demonstrating superior competency. Obviously, the awards and affirmation from her parents somehow had failed to register. She still suffers from her lack of social skills and the constant pain of feeling inferior and being laughed at by others.

Now, in this phase of life, all of that has turned around, not because she is convinced that her academic performance was worthwhile, but because she has seen the fruit of her labor. She saw that her writing had worth. Through that achievement, she went back to reevaluate the life she had lived up to this point. The critical role of her husband tremendously assisted that.

It is also important to note that before Claire achieved a sense of worth, her tolerance for her child was low. Usually people who are structured and orderly have a low tolerance for the playfulness and creativity of children; but even above that, Claire was still exhibiting the stupor of low self-esteem.

We see in Claire the miracle of a complete turnaround exhibited by that acknowledgement: "I can do something worthwhile. I can make a difference." Even further, she is enjoying a sense of personal growth. Truly, Claire's innate ability to write was there all the time. Each of us has the inherent capacity to excel at particular tasks. It wasn't important that Claire's column be syndicated. That was icing on the cake. The true acknowledgment came through seeing the work of her hand in the local paper and beginning to have a sense of accomplishment when she stepped back and looked at the finished product.

The truth of Claire Winters Sorenson needs to be a reminder to all of us. Though most of us may not have been awkward, social misfits in high school, we all know people who were. Perhaps even now as adults, the assumption continues that people have nothing to contribute. But I have witnessed many Claires, gifted individuals. All it takes is focusing their attributes and energies in the right direction, and then a bouquet bursts into full bloom, radiant with excitement and enthusiasm.

With newfound confidence and a sense of purpose, these people suddenly have time for other people, including family. Life feels worthwhile. They can make a contribution. They are fun to be around and are not a constant drain or in a state of stress. Unfortunately, such a change cannot be artificially induced by patting someone on the back and giving affirmation. The individual must have an opportunity to produce something worthwhile. On the other hand, as that individual is productive and excels, those of us standing by should be quick to give praise.

I have also seen people like Claire who did not have the benefit of a supportive spouse, people who are laboring as teachers, administrators, nurses, bank loan officers, and so forth. They appear to be pleasant, but down deep something is missing. The truth is they are most likely quite good at what they do, but they haven't put forth the energy to excel and be proud of what they do. They have made an assumption that their lives do not count. They see themselves as C+ people: They think they always have been so, are now, and always will be. That's tragic.

Logically, a person who views himself or herself as a C+ person must assume there are also A+ people, B+ people, and so forth. But somehow he or she is doomed to an eternally average life. However, I have yet—in thousands of case histories—to find a person who lacks the ability to be excellent at something, and that something is worthy of a lifetime.

As she moves to the next phase, Claire can't help but continue to grow—much the same as a tree that is growing from spring into summer. Its leaves are little buds on the branches that continue to grow until it is a huge, beautiful landmark. So will be the pattern for Claire. Interestingly, because of the despair of her earlier years, Claire will not forget to note the joy in her life, whereas many of us may take it for granted. She will never retire from growing. She will never be too old to emit her radiance to others.

Chapter 16

Flame Out

Jerry Cox

J
erry Cox no longer had enough money to buy or build a
sports camp of his own, not even a small one, but he did find
a summer camp that was in financial trouble. The board was
very interested in the potential of using his name and listened
carefully as he described an all-sports camp tailored to rehabilitate
delinquent and substance-abusing kids. The board also liked the
fact that he was willing to finance his ideas.

"How are those kinds of kids going to pay for a sports camp?"
asked a board member. "It's going to cost a lot of money to mount
a program like you want. There will be equipment costs and higher
insurance rates. I just don't know."

"I'm sure that when we demonstrate how effective a camp like
this can be," urged Jerry, "we'll have no trouble securing additional
grants from philanthropists and foundations. When I was playing

football, I participated in many promotionals and fund-raisers for charitable organizations."

Finally, after a lot of discussion, the board agreed to experiment with Jerry's idea—provided he put up the money needed to winterize the camp, purchase the equipment, and hire the staff to mount the new program. "But we're a not-for-profit corporation," said the chairman, "so we can't give you a share in the camp or anything. You'll be making a contribution, not an investment. There will be no return. We'll put you on staff—at a modest salary—but if the idea of a sports camp doesn't work out, we'll have to adjust. We've been facing the possibility of selling the camp. If your plan doesn't work, it still might come to that, and you'd get nothing out of it.

"I'm just telling you that for the record. All we can give you is the opportunity to launch a sports-camp program, since you say that's what you want to do."

Jerry was delighted, but when his wife, Lisa, heard his plan, she was dubious. "Would we have to live up there? I hate the sticks. There'd be nothing to do. Where would I shop?"

"What do you mean, you 'hate the sticks'? I met you in the mountains of Colorado!"

"That's different. Everybody was up there—the lodge, the pool, the bars—something was always happening."

"Well, come with me to see the camp. I think you'll fall in love with it."

They went to the camp that Friday, but even Jerry gulped when he saw how run-down the place was. The dining hall had a concrete floor with picnic tables covered with linoleum. The group shower rooms smelled of mildew. The bunkhouses were drafty and had tin tacked over the broken windows. There was a rough game room with a smoky fireplace, but it was a long way from being a beautiful ski-resort lodge with beamed ceiling and picture windows overlooking an alpine valley.

"This is nothing like Colorado!" Lisa fumed in disgust. "If you go through with this, you can say good-bye to me. I'm not coming anywhere near here, not even to visit."

"Come on, Lisa," Jerry begged. "I have to do this. I want to give something back to kids like me. Besides, what else am I gonna do?"

"I have no idea what you're gonna do. That's your problem. Do what you want, but I won't be part of this dump," she said, and she stalked back to the car.

A few days later when Lisa discovered that Jerry had transferred most of his assets to the camp, she exploded. "What? You just gave them the money? You can't do that! That's my money, too."

"Well, no, it wasn't," Jerry said stubbornly. "I made it, and it was always in my account. I think this is the best next step for the future. I wish you wouldn't be so upset."

"It may be the best step for your future, but I told you I'd have nothing to do with it!" stormed Lisa. "I'm getting an attorney, and we'll see if some of that money isn't mine." Within a few hours she had thrown some things in a suitcase, grabbed their son, and left the condo.

And as it turned out, her departure was permanent. She sued for divorce and got it, but she did not recover any of the money Jerry gave to the camp . . . unless the stiff alimony payments Jerry was required to pay could be counted as her share.

The divorce was a blow to Jerry, but in a way it was also a relief. Lisa had been on his back more and more during the last couple years. To compensate, Jerry threw himself 100 percent into developing the camp program.

Football was the premier sport, and football camp ran during the summer when Jerry could recruit some of the better college players from around the country to contribute a few weeks for little or no pay. He enjoyed being able to throw a football again and was very organized in using his time. Through his name and contacts, he was able to attract a lot of high school kids at risk for delinquency who aspired to bigger and better things. The program was very popular, and he felt it was truly successful because he could imagine what might otherwise have happened to those kids.

But the program was not successful in attracting more money. True delinquents—kids who had already gotten in trouble——had lost their motivation to improve their lives and didn't sign up for the camp, but without them, Jerry couldn't create the statistics to show that his camp worked. Without that proof, Jerry wasn't able to convince foundations of the merits of the camp. Therefore, he got no grants.

Still, Jerry pressed on. The key to success that he had learned in jail was to lock on a goal and focus all his energy on accomplishing it. That had worked in college ball and professional ball, so he applied it to running the camp. The only problem was, he lacked another essential talent for his position: the supervisory knack required to manage the staff.

As the camp neared the five-year mark and Jerry approached his fortieth birthday, he seemed to have less energy and patience for staff management, which he didn't particularly enjoy. More and more often he lost his temper. At first, staff members made allowances for "tough Coach Cox," but as it got worse, Jerry had a harder and harder time getting the good staff members to return.

When his temper tantrums began to focus on the kids, word went out that the sports camp was not a fun place to go. Then camp registration went down: It was blamed on the economy or inadequate publicity at first, but by the next year, the board began to suspect the real reasons. They called Jerry in and presented the facts: declining enrollment, no outside grants, and rumors that kids didn't want to come because of how "mean" Jerry could be.

"What do you mean? This is a sports camp," bristled Jerry. "We're not here to baby-sit these kids. They come to learn. Football's a tough sport, and they've got to learn to take it."

"That's not the way we see it," said one of the board members. "These kids are our customers—especially since you haven't found any grant money. I wouldn't go so far as to say that the customer is always right, but they've got to go home thinking they've had a good time. But that's not been in the reports we've been hearing."

"You've just been listening to some wimps," said Jerry defensively.

"How about your staff?" challenged another board member. "You started by getting some good people in here. But I've called a few of them, and they tell me they won't come back because you can't control your temper. What's going on?"

"Who'd you call? I'm not going to answer any questions unless I know who's making the accusations."

"It doesn't make any difference who made those comments. I consider them relevant to your effectiveness as the director," said the board member.

"What is this, anyway? I put up the money and do all the work, clean up this place, and you're talking behind my back? Is that it? Then, I'm outta here." And he stomped out of the room into the night air.

Jerry got in his Porsche—much the worse for wear by now—and spun out onto the road. The longer he drove, the angrier he got. Things just weren't working out, and it wasn't fair! Life had been cruel to him. He had no close friends anymore, no wife (well, good riddance to her), his money was gone, and now the one thing he had pinned his hopes on was going sour. It didn't help that Christmas was only a week away. *What a rotten gift*, he thought.

Now he was almost forty years old, and the one thing he had loved—football—the one thing that had been so good to him, was far in the past and there was no way to go back.

Trees and road signs flashed by in the Porsche headlights, but Jerry's mind was on autopilot. The more he thought about it, the more he began to think that the reason his football years had been so good was the money. *Was it the money, or was it the game? Or was it both?* he wondered. He wasn't sure anymore. Bitterly, he remembered how many people had tried to rip him off when he had money. But that's not the money's fault. You just can't trust people.

It really infuriated him that the sports camp wasn't working out. "The one time when I've really tried doing good for other people," he said aloud to himself as the car screeched around a turn. "And what did I get for it? No appreciation! No appreciation at all."

Jerry drove all night and arrived in San Francisco just as the sun was coming up. As he drove by Candlestick Park, he realized the 49ers were playing that day at noon. He wheeled into a parking space and found the box office. It was too early for the windows to be open, but a sign said the game was sold out. Jerry cursed as he walked around. Taking in a game would have been a way to relieve his tension.

Finally, he found a coffee shop nearby and went in for some breakfast. "Know anybody who might have some tickets for today's game?" he asked the freckle-faced kid behind the counter.

The kid called through the window to the cook. "Hey, Joe, got any tickets? There's a guy out here who wants some."

Joe came out wiping his hands on his apron. "How many you want?" he said, looking Jerry over.

"Just one. I wanna see the game."

The cook glanced around to see who else was in the shop, then said, "Eighty-five bucks."

"Eighty-five bucks! That's highway robbery!"

"Eighty-five bucks. Tickets are hard to come by, buddy. The box office sold out three weeks ago."

"How about giving me a break? I'm Jerry Cox; I used to play pro ball. How about giving me one for fifty-five?"

The cook shrugged. "Eighty-five, take it or leave it. Makes no difference to me who you were." The cook headed back toward the kitchen.

"All right, all right." Jerry got his ticket.

He had lots of time to kill before the game and spent it exploring the area on foot. Suddenly, a voice behind him said, "Hey, Cox, is that you?"

Jerry turned, thrilled that his football fame wasn't completely forgotten. But the man who had called his name was his old cell mate from the slammer. "Rico? Is it really you?"

"Yeah, man. Been a long time. Whatcha doin' 'round here?"

"Oh, I'm just gonna take in the game. How 'bout you?"

"I'm all business, man."

"Business? What business?" asked Jerry.

Rico threw his head back and studied Jerry through lowered eyelids. "I'm a runner for a numbers game. It's big, man. You wouldn't believe how much money turns over with each football game. It's better than horses or anything else. How 'bout if I give you a tip? It'll make your day, since you're going to the game. For old time's sake, ya know."

Jerry bought in for a hundred dollars, though Rico razzed him about being so light. "Man, I'm telling you, I'm offering you a solid tip. Lay some real money on me, and you can buy yourself a new car tomorrow."

"What?"

"You heard what I said."

"Sorry," said Jerry. "That's all I can afford."

"All right. Look me up after the game. I'll be at that sports bar you can see a block down there."

The 49ers won, and Jerry went to pick up his winnings.

"Hey, man, were you serious about being low on bread?" Rico queried.

"Well, yeah—at least for now. I'm a working man these days," Jerry replied, remembering even as he said it how uncertain that was. "I don't have a football salary anymore."

"Hey, that's right. You played ball for a while, didn't you?"

Jerry nodded. People just didn't remember anymore.

"Well, listen," said Rico. "I might be able to get you in on a good deal here, if you're interested. This is a sure thing, man. And you might have the football savvy we could use."

Jerry listened as Rico talked about the numbers racket. "Of course, the boss will have to approve you and everything, but I'll put in a good word for you."

That afternoon, Jerry headed back to the sports camp. He was going to pack his things and start a new life. *What the heck*, he thought. *It can't be any worse than things have been for me here lately.*

Up to this point, Jerry has had his ups and downs. He had the relatively rare experience of achieving excellence and dramatic financial success early in life. However, as I have studied people's lives, I find that very few can sustain their early fame or fortune unless they are able to reposition to a field that allows them to continue to grow according to their aptitude strengths.

In the case of professional athletes, they need to make a transition to another field that utilizes different aptitudes than their declining physical talents. Jerry, like many who face the end of a golden era, attempts to borrow the status and the skills of his athletic glory and apply them in a related field.

But athletes aren't the only people who struggle with adjustment after early success. I have seen managers, sales personnel, teachers, accountants, and many others who experienced a boom time early in life but come to the end of their line when their company is sold or a new president comes in. Rather than reevaluate their circumstances, they just plow ahead trying to reproduce the good times of the past.

Each of us is gifted with sufficient capacity to succeed in more than one career or occupation. A master carpenter who loses his right arm in a work injury is not all washed up. The aptitudes that enabled him to be a master carpenter can be transferred to other fields. In addition, he has other capacities that, if identified and focused, can be developed to a master's level.

In the case of Jerry Cox, he tried to continue in the limelight of his football career by assuming that he could manage a camp. It was a desperate attempt to preserve the past. Jerry would have been better served to have discovered the full range of his aptitude strengths above and beyond his athletic capacity and contributed those to helping delinquent kids.

For football players, the statistics are staggering. The average professional football player is broke and divorced within two years after hanging up his cleats.

It's not that they lack other talents. But at first their phone is always ringing. There is always somebody with a new deal who leads the athlete to believe that there is another mountaintop in their athletic career that will put them back in the fast lane again. But each new deal takes considerable expense and lasts from three to six months to investigate and try out. As the athlete goes from deal to deal, there isn't the refocusing of their aptitudes and the pursuit of their next career. There is aimless going from one project to another until the money is all gone and the friends as well.

If Jerry doesn't soon discover a vocation that fits his talents, he may not be able to pull himself out of this downward spiral.

Accelerated Performance or Devastation

I n phase four a person has definitely entered "middle age"—
the period typically covering the ages of forty to fifty-five. Here
we find individuals riding the crest of the wave, enjoying the
fruit of their hard work of earlier years. A person who is
enjoying "success" in a job suited to his or her talent strengths has
also had to learn how to navigate all the other bumps in the road
of life—how to get along with difficult people, how to compromise
without getting walked over, how to overcome disappointments
and handle conflict, how to manage money, the value of trusted
relationships.

This is also the age when people begin to face their mortality,
however. Children of middle-agers are going to college and place
a drain on finances; aging parents need more care; retirement looms

around the corner. Some may realize they are stuck in unsuitable jobs, but fear makes them hang on to a guaranteed income or pension plan. Others may have learned some of life's hard lessons but still don't know how to put them into action. For those who are "stuck," life begins to deteriorate into disappointment.

In this chapter we meet our five friends coming together once more for their thirtieth high school reunion. Listen in as, in their own words, they review the roads their lives have taken. How does each one feel about himself or herself at this point? What degree of satisfaction or dissatisfaction do they express? Are they able to be honest with their old classmates—or are they still fooling themselves? Most importantly, in what ways does their experience resonate with crossroads you are facing?

If you have not reached this phase, think ahead as to how you can avoid the pitfalls and plan for the plums.

Chapter 17

The Class Reunion

Diana Slater Barber picked up her hotel room phone for the umpteenth time. It was a good thing the Waterston Motor Inn allowed free local calls, or she would have gone over her budget for the thirtieth reunion of Cascade High School's class of '68.

At noon, Robert Wilford would pick her up and take her to the airport to meet with the other two members of the planning committee to finalize the details for the reunion. Phil Grady was arriving on a 12:08 flight from LAX. Claire Winters Sorenson was driving in.

Earlier in the spring, the chairperson from the class's twenty-fifth reunion had called Diana. "It's my job to pass on the torch for our thirtieth class reunion," the woman had said over the phone. "So, I was wondering whether you would take over. For our tenth and twentieth we used the class officers and a few other people—you didn't attend, did you?"

"No," said Diana. "I was too busy—family, new career. You know."

"Well, we used up all the class officers, so for the thirtieth, we're calling on other people. You know, people who were somebody. And since you were voted the girl 'Most Likely to Succeed,' I'm asking you. Would you be willing to chair the committee?"

The idea interested Diana. It would be nice to see her old classmates again and find out how they were doing. "Who else is on the committee?" she asked.

"Up to you. You're the first person I called. But you might try Robert Wilford—you remember him, don't you? He was the guy 'Most Likely to Succeed,' and he hasn't done anything for a reunion yet. We usually have had a committee of four."

Diana agreed, especially if she could put together her own committee. "Can you send me a list of addresses and phone numbers?"

"Sure, and I'll mark those who've already served on a committee."

Robert Wilford said yes, but Diana had to consult her yearbook to remind herself of some of the other people. She tried Marilyn York, the yearbook editor, but Marilyn lived too far away. "Have you tried Phil Grady?" she inquired. "He might be a good person. He designed the yearbook, you know."

Phil agreed, but after several more calls Diana was running out of names and was about to go with a committee of three when she noticed in the yearbook that Claire Winters, their valedictorian, had not yet been checked off the list. She ought to be a good candidate, thought Diana.

Claire made their fourth committee member.

Robert thought a planning meeting with everyone present was unnecessary. "We still have two months before the homecoming reunions in October," he said. "Can't we do everything over a conference call? I'd be glad to go over to Waterston and do some of the legwork. My folks still live there, you know. And I'm only an hour away."

But as chairperson for the committee, Diana wanted to check out all the arrangements for the reunion personally and see that the guest list was complete. She was sure Robert could have done a good job, but she had been asked to chair the committee, and she knew enough about committees to know that the people on site were the people with the most to say about decisions. Just by being in town since the night before, Diana had checked out dozens of details herself. She felt competent going to the meeting with informed recommendations.

The other committee members had been glad to come at their own expense. "It'll be a minireunion in itself!" said Phil Grady on the phone. "I haven't seen any of you guys since high school, even though I lived in Waterston a while after I got out of the service."

It has been said that at high school reunions (especially of twenty-five years or more) people discover that their classmates' appearances have changed tremendously, but Diana was surprised at how much Robert looked like his old self. His hair was receding and he was pudgy around the middle, but she could have picked him out of any crowd.

"Diana, you look great!" Robert said with his familiar hundred-watt smile when she climbed into the black Lexus. Her dark hair was streaked with gray, but she felt it added an air of professionalism, and she was glad that she had worked hard to recover a healthy figure after the births of her four children.

"You said on the phone that you only lived an hour away from Waterston," said Diana as they drove toward the airport. "But wasn't your dad's company right here in town, an electronics company or something out on Riverside Drive?"

"Yeah, that's where it was—still is, as a matter of fact. But I don't work there anymore."

"I thought you were in line to take over from your father."

"You and everybody else thought the same thing—even me. And I did take over, or at least I tried. I was president for several years and almost ran the company into the ground before I realized I wasn't the corporate-president type."

"You could have fooled me," said Diana. "After all, you were named 'Most Likely to Succeed' back in '68, weren't you?"

"Yeah, and so were you."

They both laughed; then Diana brushed her hand across the padded leather dashboard of the fine car. "Well, it looks like you're doing pretty well."

"Oh, the car? It's my dad's. My car is in the shop today. I did okay once I got pointed in the right direction. But the going was mighty rough for a while."

"What are you doing now?"

"I'm president of the Boys and Girls Society," Robert said as he turned into the airport parking lot and took the time card from the meter.

"The B-G Society? I've heard of that agency," said Diana with surprise. "That's quite a group, as I recall. How'd you get there? I never thought of you as the association type. I always saw you as the businessman."

"Well, that's a long story. I think that image was what I wanted people to think—what I thought myself at the time, I guess. But no, I'm not a businessman in the traditional sense. It's my job to represent the agency to the public. I speak, raise money, help recruit volunteers . . . that kind of thing. I'm kind of a glorified PR man with a title. But the best part is that I don't have to manage the agency. Our executive vice president, Herb Olden, does that, and he's great."

"You're kidding! You gave up control?"

"Yes and no. The amazing thing is, these have been my real strengths all my life. Everyone just assumed that because I got along so well with people, could make convincing presentations, and promote projects or ideas effectively, I was suited to run a manufacturing company. What I didn't realize was that I also had a strong urge to reassure and support people."

"Well, what's wrong with that? That sounds commendable."

Robert finished parking and they both got out before he answered. "Nothing wrong with it, and in my current job I can make good use of those talents. But when I was the president of Wilford Electronics, those concerns made it difficult for me to make the hard personnel and management decisions that are usually needed to run most any operation."

They arrived early at the gate for Phil Grady's plane and sat down to wait. Diana was curious: "How'd you find out about this mismatch between you and your job?"

"I felt like I was going down for the third time before I got any help," Robert said, trying to get comfortable in the airport lounge seat. "Problems began to show up when I was vice president of marketing and sales, but I just worked harder to meet expectations—mine and everyone else's. My marriage began to suffer, and I nearly lost my wife. We worked it out, but I felt terrible; I didn't know what to do. Then when I became president, I was faced with management decisions that I had avoided or made poorly until the company almost went bankrupt. My dad would have lost everything if it hadn't been for the help of some creative attorneys. That's when I got out of the business and they hired a president better suited for the job."

"That's an incredible story," Diana marveled. "But how did you become president of the B-G Society, of all things?"

Robert smiled. "It's kind of ironic, really. My mother had often encouraged me to become a minister, but I'd always brushed off the idea. But when things fell apart at Wilford Electronics, I went to my pastor and asked what he thought about my doing something for people. Over the years he became a trusted counselor and got to know me very well. After asking a few more questions about what had happened at Wilford, he said that going to seminary might be a good idea—but not to study for the ministry. I had no idea what he had in mind, but a few days later he called and told me that he had a friend on the board at the B-G Society and they were looking for someone just like me. I couldn't believe it. But as it turned out, they had all the doctorates they needed; what they didn't have was someone to do what I'm doing now. . . . . Hey, I think that's the plane."

The Boeing 747 nosed into the terminal and the passengers began filing out of the gate. Phil Grady wasn't hard to spot. Soon all three '68 graduates were shaking hands and laughing self-consciously over one another's similarity to their old yearbook photos. But no one mentioned the slight limp they'd noticed when Phil walked through the aisle.

At the airport restaurant, they found that Claire Winters Sorenson had already reserved a table for them. "Diana! Robert!" The journalist greeted them, smiling warmly. Then she laughed. "And Phil Grady! I remember you. We crashed in the lunchroom the day the yearbooks were given out."

"No!" Phil laughed. "You're kidding me."

Diana was surprised at how friendly and at ease Claire seemed. The Claire Winters she remembered from the yearbook picture had been a mousy sort of person who did little more than study all the time. *It's strange how people blossom when they mature*, she thought. *But then, I didn't know her very well.*

The afternoon passed quickly as the committee went over the details of the class reunion and made decisions about where it would be held, the food, the entertainment, a band. Diana was glad she had done as much advance research as she had.

Finally, Diana passed out the address list of '68 alumni. The whereabouts of thirteen graduates were either unknown to the school office or the initial announcements sent to the last address had been returned "addressee unknown."

"All right," said Diana, "with the next mailing, let's list these alumni we can't find and have people phone us if they know where they are."

"Sounds like a good idea," said Robert.

Claire studied the list. "What about Jerry Cox?" she said. "Someone has to know where he is. He was a professional football player for many years, wasn't he?"

"His mom lived here in Waterston back when I was in the fire department here in town," said Phil Grady. "Claire, if you would give me a ride in your car, we could go over to her place and see if she knows where he is."

The committee took a break, agreeing to meet back at Diana's hotel for dinner. "I think we can finish during dinner and still get Phil back here to meet his 9:38 flight," Diana said.

Once Phil and Claire were gone, Robert turned to Diana. "You got my saga on the way over here, but I haven't heard your story. What happened to that older guy you were going with—Greg somebody—the one who was going to be a doctor?"

"It didn't work out with him," Diana shrugged. "Probably all for the better. I went to Mid-Valley State and met a guy headed for seminary. Jim and I fell in love rather quickly and have had a good life. We have four children; two are twins." She rummaged in her purse and produced a family portrait photo. "This is somewhat dated but it's my favorite picture. It was funny listening to your story," she mused, toying with her coffee cup, "because in some ways my husband, Jim, had a similar experience. He was ordained after seminary and took a very promising church. Things went well at first, but then he butted heads with the chairman of the board. In time we had to admit that Jim didn't have much talent for managing people, either. As a matter of fact, I was the manager, and I made matters worse by trying to manage the church by proxy through him." She gave a short, embarrassed laugh. "What he was good at was preaching, and finally he negotiated a way to preach without fighting with the chairman of the board, who—when allowed to have his hand—has proven to be very capable in guiding the church."

"What happened to you, then?" asked Robert. "Were you relegated to 'managing' the home?"

Diana made a wry face. "A home with four kids is a challenge for anyone to manage! And for several years, I home schooled them too . . . but in time, things got rough for me. I actually ended up going to see a psychologist. She said nothing was wrong with me; I just needed to find an appropriate outlet for my management aptitude."

The waiter came by for the third time asking if there was anything more they wanted and making it obvious that he wanted them to vacate their table.

When they had retrieved Robert's car from the parking lot and were heading back into town, he asked, "So what, besides this alumni reunion committee, have you found to manage, Miss Most Likely to Succeed?"

Seeing that he had said it in truly good humor, she grinned imp ishly. "Well, I've been looking for a position as the president of an electronics firm. Got any suggestions?" They both laughed.

Then Diana got serious. "What I actually found fits me perfectly: I'm the director of a day school. I'd always enjoyed our own kids, but what really interests me most is making the school run properly. I actually enjoy planning the fund-raising events, recruiting volunteers, working with the staff, even fighting with the city council when zoning issues come up. That kind of thing drives most people crazy, but I eat it up."

"Doesn't running a day school take some special type of training or something?"

"Yes. My undergraduate degree was in early childhood development. But I went back to school for my master's in administration.

And it's been invaluable. It gives me the credentials necessary to deal with the public."

"That's interesting. I almost went back to school to get an MBA not long after I was promoted to sales manager at Wilford Electronics. I was foundering, and more school seemed like a lifeboat."

"That's not a very good reason to go back to school," said Diana. "You need to be suited for the job; then school adds skills, confidence, and knowledge to help you do it better. School can never make you what you're not."

"Yeah. I finally realized that. I was lucky I didn't waste my time and money on it."

Robert guided the car off the expressway and then changed the subject. "Mind if I ask you a personal question?"

Diana glanced at him. "Go ahead. If it's too personal, I'll just say so; I won't be offended."

"Well," said Robert thoughtfully, "with you being the managing type, how do you work out roles in your family? I mean, it doesn't sound like you and Jim could have a very traditional marriage. So what is it—egalitarian? Or do you 'wear the pants,' so to speak?"

Diana nodded. It was a fair question. A lot of water had gone under the bridge . . . but she gave it a shot.

"When the kids were little," she said, thinking back, "I could pour all my energy into them, but as I got older I found it harder and harder for all my capacity to be absorbed in home management. I no longer felt like I was able to contribute anything significant. I wasn't doing anything. I'm not putting down homemaking. But that just wasn't enough for me to do, so no matter how much I applied myself, it didn't help me grow in using my supervisory capacities."

She sighed. "That's when I began getting Jim in trouble with the church. I could see all the politics going on, and I would nudge him to say this or do that or watch out for some person. Well, he admitted that I was a super sleuth, but when he tried to pull it off, the situation often blew up."

"But what happened in your marriage roles?"

"I'm coming to that. When I saw the problems my advice caused, I tried to hold back. That was good for Jim but bad for me. I became pretty hard to live with. I was snapping at everyone, especially the kids. That's when I went to a counselor. If I hadn't, our marriage might not have survived.

"When we got a better handle on my restlessness, Jim and I talked through what it meant for him to be the head of our family when I had the better management aptitude. There are a lot of things that I take the lead on even though Jim carries the ultimate responsibility for our family's welfare, spiritual direction, and values. After all, there's more to being a good husband and father than managing people. And it doesn't negate my function of managing to operate in a context of submission."

"That's very interesting," said Robert as he pulled up in front of the Motor Inn. "There's been so much fighting between 'traditional' and 'liberated' camps that marriage roles usually get painted in overly simplistic terms. On one hand, traditionalists say that the husband's role and the wife's role should only be a certain way. On the other hand, the 'liberated' woman wouldn't be caught dead saying or doing anything that smacks of submission. But you and Jim seem to be creative in blending traditional roles and your personal gifts."

Diana smiled at the compliment as she got out of the car. Robert agreed to be back at the motel for dinner . . . after he picked up his own car and returned his father's Lexus.

On their way over to Mrs. Cox's house, Claire asked Phil what he'd been doing since he was in the fire department. "I noticed that you have a slight limp. Did you get injured fire fighting?"

Phil shook his head and found himself telling Claire about his accident and subsequent discovery of a more creative career in filmmaking in the Los Angeles area. "There was a point in my life when everything was working well, Angela and I were happy, and there wasn't anything we really needed." He shrugged. "But then I got greedy."

"What do you mean? You don't look like the greedy type."

"Oh, it wasn't money so much. It had to do with trying to make my work situation perfect. I wasn't willing to let well enough alone. The more I got in touch with the things I liked and didn't like to do, the more I tried to engineer my job into perfection. . . . Oh, turn at the next right."

Claire made the turn and drove silently as Phil went on.

"I was hired to advise the studio on anything related to fire-fighters. I was also supposed to inform them about fire-safety matters on the sets. Most of my work allowed me to be as creative as I could be, especially where firefighters were concerned in any movie or television show, but part of my job involved keeping current on fire codes and safety standards. That was the part I didn't like.

"At the same time I was getting feelers from other studios suggesting that I could get better deals with them, so I thought I was in the catbird seat and started throwing my weight around by saying 'I won't do this' and 'I won't do that.'

"Before I knew what had happened, I was fired."

"You got fired? Didn't they give you any kind of warning or anything?"

"Oh, there were warnings if I would've paid attention, but no one actually said, 'If you don't cool it, we're going to let you go.'"

"I guess it was a good thing you had those other offers," Claire noted.

"That's what I thought, but once I was on my own, I discovered they weren't such solid offers; they were just 'inquiries.' That really threw me for a loop. I started getting very down on myself. I began wondering whether I was being punished for trying to be creative and going against my parents' style. Angela said that was foolishness, that I should look at how happy I had been for several years when I found the kind of job I liked. 'You just tried to push it too far,' she said. 'Even a bed of roses has its thorns. Everybody's got to live with them.' It was hard to admit it, but she was right, you know. . . . Uh, it's the next left, I think."

Claire flicked the left turn signal.

"Finally, I did get an offer—for the job I have now," Phil said. "It's even a little better than the one I got fired from, but more importantly, I've learned that the best I should expect a job to be is for about 60 percent of my time to be spent in my niche. That leaves 40 percent for red tape, hassles, boredom . . . whatever.

"Angela is a registered nurse, and during a seminar she learned the 60/40 principle. It helped me find my place. If, during about 60 percent of the time, a person isn't doing what he or she likes and has a real talent for doing, then that person's in the wrong job. That's the way I was at the fire department. Fire calls and a few other things were okay, but that constituted only about 10 or 15 percent of my time, and I was miserable.

"However, as Angela said, every job has its thorns, and if you try to push your contentment level above 60 percent, you might be asking for an unrealistic world."

"Sounds like you were going for an 80/20 world, and it just didn't exist," observed Claire.

"You got it," said Phil as they stopped in front of the house where Mrs. Cox lived.

A haggard woman in her seventies answered the door. "Yes," she said tentatively through the screen.

"I'm Phil Grady, and this is Claire Sorenson. We're old high school classmates of Jerry's. Are you Mrs. Cox?"

"Yes," she said again in the same uncertain way.

"We're trying to find Jerry to invite him to our thirtieth class reunion," said Claire. "Do you know where we could reach him?"

"Oh . . . I don't think he'd be interested in coming."

"But could you give us his address or phone number so we could ask him?"

"Well, I . . . " The old woman seemed to choke up. "I don't really know where he is these days."

"What was his last address? Maybe he's left forwarding information," said Claire.

"Ohh," moaned the woman behind the screen. Her hand came to her mouth as she turned away from the door and shuffled back into the dimly lit room.

Phil looked at Claire and shrugged, his eyebrows arching in surprise.

When Claire looked through the screen door, she could see the woman standing in the middle of the room with her back to them. Great sobs seemed to be shaking her tired body. "Do you mind if we come in?" asked Claire as gently as possible. One hand went up, and the woman waved them in with an air of resignation.

Inside, she pointed toward a tattered sofa while she rummaged among the things piled high on the table until she produced a box of tissues. She pulled three out and began dabbing her eyes as she lowered herself into a straight-backed chair.

"What's happened?" urged Phil. "Last I heard, Jerry was a football star."

"He was," replied Mrs. Cox. "Then he worked for a few years at that sports camp. He seemed really happy. Then they said that one day he just packed up all his things and left. No one knew why, or at least they didn't tell me." A long sigh escaped from the old woman.

"The next time I heard from Jerry was when he sent me a money order for three thousand dollars. 'Just thought you could use it, Mom,' was all the note said. It wasn't even a check; it was a money order, and he didn't give me his address, though the postmark said San Francisco. It was like he just faded away. I don't know what's become of him."

"You mean you haven't heard from him since?" asked Claire incredulously.

"Only once," said Mrs. Cox, her lip trembling. "I got this letter from a Chaplain William Carter of the Union Gospel Mission in San Francisco. He explained that when men stay overnight at the mission, he encourages them to write to someone they love. Apparently, Jerry started writing to me . . . then just got up and walked out of the mission."

"Was there anything else?" Phil encouraged.

"There was one piece of smudged stationery with just a few words on it. It said, 'Dear Mom, Sorry I haven't written before, but I didn't know what to say,' and that was the end."

"Did you try to find out more?"

Mrs. Cox nodded. "Yes. I called the mission. I had to call three or four times before I got through to Chaplain Carter. He remembered Jerry and said he looked fairly good for . . . for someone . . . living on the street." Mrs. Cox shuddered involuntarily and tears spilled down her cheeks. Phil and Claire waited patiently as the old woman composed herself.

"But the chaplain had no idea where he was," she finally continued. "He said Jerry's never come back to that mission. He promised he would do his best to get in touch with me if Jerry ever showed up again."

The old woman took a deep breath and lifted her chin. "And that's all I know about my Jerry. I'm sorry I can't help you."

Phil and Claire tried to murmur words of comfort to the old woman before they left, but they had no idea what to say. In a few minutes they said good-bye and drove silently to Diana's hotel.

That evening when all the plans for the reunion had been completed and Robert had volunteered to drive Phil to the airport, Claire asked if she could stay a while and talk to Diana.

"Were you sort of religious in high school?" she asked frankly. "I seem to remember something like that."

"Yes," Diana smiled. "In fact, I still am."

"Good. Then maybe you can help me with something."

"I'm not sure, but I'll try."

"I've been asked to write a book about the movie industry," said Claire in a lowered voice, as though she were revealing some trade secret or a great embarrassment.

"Why, that's great," Diana said. "I always read your column. I appreciate how you've been including more criticism of movie morality—or immorality, as it so often is. I think that's good."

"That's just the point," Claire said. "I've been reviewing movies for years now, and I'm increasingly concerned with the lack of moral tone. It's not just the sex and violence. Even when someone is compassionate and caring, it's done impulsively, not as a result of any compelling worldview. I get the feeling that the only nice people in the movies are those the producers want the audience to like. It's that shallow."

"You've mentioned those ideas in some of your columns," Diana noted.

"Yes, but do you know what kind of criticism I get back from Hollywood? I get the same amoral line thrown around in so many movies: Who am I to question anybody's morality?"

"How do you answer that?"

Claire frowned. "That's why I asked if you were religious. I've become convinced that if it's left up to me, then I don't have a right to question another person's morality—whether it's private or portrayed all over a movie screen. But I've been thinking . . . for society to hold together, there has to be something beyond ourselves."

A small smile played on Diana's mouth.

"I think about that with my son, Kevin," Claire continued seriously. "He's a teenager and so he naturally pulls away from me and his father. What we say seems to count very little, if at all. He's trying to become his own person. What we need is some standard of good and evil, some measure of truth beyond ourselves toward which we can point him. But all he hears and sees tells him it's everyone for himself or herself."

"So, you're starting to wonder if that's the role of religion," observed Diana.

"Right. And remembering that you were religious, I thought I'd ask you. You know, that's another thing about the movies. They seldom portray religion as a basis for rational thought or behavior for the average person."

"But isn't that logical?" Diana said. "If Hollywood is interested in portraying life without morals, then it would be counterproductive to depict religious people in a positive light."

"I'm sure you're right, and that's what I intend to deal with in my book. But I wonder if you could suggest something I could read that would illustrate religious morality at its best."

"Why not the Bible?"

"That's pretty broad. Where would I begin?"

"Try Jesus and His Sermon on the Mount in the New Testament Book of Matthew for a remarkable review of morality. Come on up to my hotel room, and I'll show you where to find that in the Bible. Of course, the Ten Commandments are pretty central, too. Then you might want to read the Gospel of John."

Later that night, after Claire left, Diana decided she would keep in touch with Claire. She certainly was a much more open and interesting person than Diana had remembered from high school. Besides, her interest in religion as a "basis for rational thought and behavior" just might lead to something more personal.

Heightened Performance or Bitterness

P eople enter phase five at around age fifty to fifty-five. By this time, it is to be hoped that individuals have found their niche and are recognized as "experts" in their field—whether that is marriage counseling or growing vegetables or selling real estate. If not, this last stage may be characterized by depression or bitterness for the rest of one's life.

Some who did not find their niche in a career per se, however, may find the retirement years providing new opportunities to use their natural talents in fulfilling ways: more time to pursue hobbies and special interests, volunteering with service organizations, or time to give to ministry. For those of us still looking ahead, the last phase of life does not have to be a twilight zone but a rewarding time of reaping the dividends of how we've invested our natural strengths and talents. Those golden years can still hold significant opportunities for growth and, even more, for the encouragment of others.

Let's take a quick glimpse at what lies in store for our five friends as they anticipate this last phase of life. And maybe we can learn from their experience.

Chapter 18

Enjoying the "Overdrive Years"

It is time to release our five Cascade High School alumni to reap the results of their life choices, but it is possible to predict with some certainty what is in store for them. Barring some unforeseen intrusion or intervention, these people will experience the fifth phase of their life—that period between ages fifty and beyond—along the tracks they have already chosen. What will it be: heightened performance and satisfaction or depressing bitterness and stagnation?

Those who have found their places and who have mastered their trades will enjoy the appreciation and respect of their peers. Often, they will appear to surf effortlessly on the crest of a wave that younger people can't even see. This is because they are not striving to do or be something for which they have no natural talents. For them these are the "overdrive years" when they go farther with less effort.

A good example of a person who had achieved this is W. Philip Keller, a man well beyond sixty-five years of age, a wildlife photographer, agronomist, and author of more than forty books. He is best known for, *A Shepherd Looks at Psalm Twenty-three*, with over two million copies in print. In several publications, including his auto-biography, he tells how pain and frustration in his life have impacted him; yet, because his purpose is clear and his life is in order, he can still smile serenely and have the energy to be available to others, as well as sense that his life has had meaning and purpose.

A contrast to Philip Keller is another person I know, a woman past the age of sixty-five who seems to find it difficult to maintain a relationship with almost anyone without some twinge of bitter-ness, complaint, or fault. Whether it is a short conversation in per-son or over the telephone, this woman always seems to feel a need to be a wet blanket to those around her. She continually complains about her physical ailments, which to her appear paramount but are no more than everyday health concerns. She has been ostra-cized by her family and lives in an illusion that fame and fortune are just around the corner as long as she travels in the right circles and is seen with the right people. Hers is a sad example of a life that could have had tremendous meaning, purpose, and contribu-tion to society and yet resulted in a person that most people avoid.

People like Philip Keller will have the energy to help others less fortunate than themselves and the optimism to survive the lumps and bumps of life that continue to come their way. They will pass down enthusiasm to their children and grandchildren. They can infect those around them with an uncanny energy and drive, though their own bodies are declining physically.

We all dream of enjoying this reward in our senior years, but those who have not found their place in life will have trouble expe-riencing it. Not everyone looks back and counts his or her life a fruitful one. With sour resignation, some endure their senior years bitter and depressed, believing they received a raw deal from life.

This is not to say that by phase five everyone is locked into suf-fering the consequences or enjoying rewards of earlier choices. As long as life lasts, change is possible. If you are at or nearing phase five you still can make a change for the better.

Jerry Cox

With Jerry Cox, for instance, there is always the hope he will experience something that will arrest his tailspin. Admittedly, the longer he persists in his destructive direction, the more difficult it will be for him to break out. As I have witnessed too many downward-spiraling lives, I have found that only something supernatural can break the deadlock. It starts with a willingness to seek help. I believe it would take help from God to alter Jerry's life permanently.

I believe Jerry's plight goes far deeper than just finding the "right" job that would finally use his natural talents. He needs a completely new orientation—in spiritual terms, a new life. Short of that, his life is likely to end prematurely on skid row or at best be endured in shiftless bitterness. What a tragic comedown for someone who soared so high, so quickly, in such a competitive field.

The story of Jerry's life shouldn't discourage us, but it should provide a sober reminder of the importance of the choices we make in life. Jerry was not just a gifted kid whose broken home and rough background were tragically too difficult to overcome. He was not merely a victim of circumstances. At many times he made real choices, some of which proved costly.

The difference between the obvious consequences he is suffering and those that a more "privileged" person would experience after making similar decisions is only superficial. Robert Wilford, for instance, also experienced "success" at an early age by inheriting an important position in his father's company. But Robert very nearly destroyed that legacy. Possibly his father's intervention or the family's wealth might have insulated him from some outward evidence of the disaster, but that does not mean he would have been a happier person than Jerry had he not taken steps to regain control of his life.

In today's society, people often forget or dismiss responsibility for the choices they make. We tend to view such people as victims worthy of pity, though not respect: We respect someone who fails and then owns up to it with remorse.

"Turning over a new leaf" can have some major consequences. I should know. It happened to me—early in my life, fortunately, at the age of twenty-one. I was diagnosed with ulcers and was very confused about my life direction. Depression had been an unwelcome companion for too many years. I still remember the clear decision I made to turn over a new leaf—in fact, to surrender control of my life to Jesus Christ who promised to give me a purpose and direction. I realized then that during those years of aimless wandering I had been spiritually dead, separated from God. My real quest was seeking fulfillment, not through the worldly success I wanted so badly, but just to be accepted by my Creator, the God of the Holy Scriptures. Since He made me, ultimately He knew the best plan for the use of my time and talents.

I belive Jerry is spiritually dead, enduring an existence separated from God. One might refer to Jerry's later life as a living "hell," the total opposite of goodness, mercy, and kindness. Ironically, for a brief time Jerry sought to help others, to help the less fortunate turn their lives around, and yet even he fell to the very state of those he wished to help. Trying to "do good" did not change who he was. I believe that doing should be an outgrowth or characteristic of being. Many people get the two reversed and think that if they just do a few more good deeds—serve others, accomplish greater achievements—they will feel accepted and complete. Jerry achieved the pinnacle of his ambitions and spent his talents serving others, but in the end, it had not changed who he was.

Yes, through good counseling Jerry could choose to turn his life around, but now that he has hit bottom, I believe there will be a yearning, an emptiness that good counseling and sober living won't fill.

Robert Wilford

Though Robert Wilford went into a tailspin even earlier in life than Jerry did, Robert did not crash. At this advanced stage in his life, he represents the master craftsperson. He has found his place: his marriage and time for his family fit well with his job; he is not sacrificing them for the sake of his career. More importantly, he seems to be at peace with his Creator. He is not preoccupied with trying to make God do something for him.

In his early years, Robert gave a false impression of success. He appeared to have it together and, indeed, was voted "Most Likely to Succeed" in high school, and yet everything came tumbling down around him. But the qualities that gained him his high school vote of affirmation had very little to do with his current success. On the outside, he had the facade of a successful person, but he was not using his innate talents, those provided by his Creator. If he had not searched for and found them, the trouble that descended on him could have led to tragic disillusionment, stagnation, perhaps even bitterness. Fortunately, he appears to have avoided that.

Robert's success interacting with people goes beyond his Multi-Relational talent in the sense that there is a depth of maturity to him that is genuinely attractive to people. Perhaps this is more the result of spiritual growth than a career/talent adjustment. Maybe we're seeing in Robert's life some of what the Bible describes as the "fruit of the Spirit." (This term, "fruit of the Spirit," is found in Galatians 5:22 and 23.) The more people get to know the mature Robert, the more they look beyond the man and see God's work in him. Isn't it a thrilling quest to experience the Creator of the universe working in us, rounding off the rough edges?

One challenge remains for Robert: Has he learned from his own experience so he won't make the same mistake with his daughter that his father made with him? Will he let his child be her own person, or will he expect her to be a chip off the old block? Undoubtedly he and his daughter will have some qualities in common, but they will most likely be very different and have varying natural talents.

The job in which Robert is now thriving and is so at peace with would have frustrated his father to no end because his father needed to wield authority, and Robert's position as president of the B-G Society includes very little supervisory authority. He's more of a public relations person. Robert's child is likely to be as different from him as he was from his father . . . though possibly in other ways. If his daughter is bright and energetic, however, she may pick up many skills that seem to duplicate Robert's and his wife's talents or those of other people they respect. But Robert must remember that his offspring was crafted by God and needs to find her own inherent direction. If he can do that, he will pass on to her a most valuable legacy.

Diana Slater Barber

With Diana, we see a very interesting paradox. Typically, people with a talent for supervising others (either the Initiating/Developing talent or the Managing talent, as described in Appendix A) become authoritarian or abrasively assertive in their day-to-day interactions with other people. But Diana—although she is a forthright, decisive individual—seems to be sensitive and considerate of others as demonstrated in how she led the committee for the class reunion and how she and her husband have been able to work out a congenial way of handling the leadership matters in their family.

Remember also how Diana chose to stop manipulating her husband and trying to express her management talents vicariously through his role as pastor of the church? Something supernatural happened to her even before she found her own outlet for her natural talents. She became free from the need to exercise her talent to affirm herself. Somehow, she established her identity apart from proving herself. Now, she is 100 percent who she is and has made appropriate choices to carry out her role within the circumstances that she finds herself.

In terms of her marriage to someone who isn't a better "manager" than she is, she understands the limitations of her situation and yet flourishes in that setting. She thrives where others might complain of being confined. She is in control, defining a zone in which she can blossom without displacing those around her. We do not see the bitterness or anger of a frustrated woman who cannot reach her full potential. We do not see a split family where she demanded to have her way and thus ran into conflict with her husband's plans and objectives.

Similarly, we do not see her manipulating friends who are less assertive. She isn't caught in a cycle where she walks away from undesirable situations only to begin another one that is equally problematic.

Phil Grady

When Phil was a firefighter, he tried to live according to a set of standards and habits that were imposed on him—even though they were contrary to his nature. His son by his first marriage experienced Phil as an irritable father who always argued with his mother. At that point, Phil was trying to pass on the rigid standards of "a place for everything, and everything in its place" without even the appreciation his parents felt for that rule of life. It made for an astringent, humorless home for Phil's first son.

But Phil's second son (from his marriage with Angela) experienced very little, if any, of this rigidity. Is that much change adequately explained by Phil's finding the right job, even one in which he could exercise his natural creativity and be done with the insistence on having "a place for everything, and everything in its place"?

I don't think so. His general peace with himself goes beyond having that "good" job. The bruises and the pains of life will continue for Phil just like they do for all of us, and yet his capacity to cope is different. He now sees his purpose in life as something greater than another weekend fishing trip or even the making of another prizewinning film. He has a new vision for what it means to become a master craftsperson.

And yet, one of the disappointments Phil will probably have to continue enduring is the fact that his parents still do not acknowledge him for who and what he is. Throughout the remainder of their lives, it is likely that they will continue to wish that he had turned out differently. When they visit Phil's home on vacation, they will not find it "satisfactory." They may even hint—none too subtly—that he should "straighten up the tools in his garage" or express their lifestyle in some other way. They may complain that he seems too loose or too laid-back, not the way they taught him to be.

It will be important for Phil to realize that, at one level—no matter what he does—his parents will not understand him. If he can accept that and love them anyway, their rigidity and inability to appreciate him will bother him less. There are other people who do understand him . . . his wife, for instance. She has been a true blessing to him, supporting him as he is.

I also believe that Phil still needs to reckon with the spiritual side of life. Although he has found his place in the expression of his natural talents, he will still have a yearning inside for meaning and purpose to the overall drama of his life.

Claire Winters Sorenson

Claire looked forward to the class reunion as an opportunity to prove to her old classmates that she was not really the misfit they thought she was back in high school. Actually, she anticipated that her accomplishments would far outshine those of the "lesser students" who used to laugh at her.

What she did not realize was that her pain had been accelerated by self-imposed fears. True, she was not the campus belle, and she did get slighted and laughed at from time to time, but a lot more cruelty and ridicule is hurled around between kids than is genuinely intended to be. Somehow Claire wouldn't brush it off like the others did. Unfortunately, Claire's fear of others trained her classmates to treat her in an adversarial way, thus further compounding the situation. Her deflated basketball would not bounce back when thrown on the floor.

At the reunion, Claire wanted to assert herself as someone who had dramatically succeeded, and she did. The new Claire with her doctorate and her writing success certainly was not the old misfit Claire.

Claire is a good example of the modern person who has made it on his or her own by sheer grit and the good fortune of finding an affirming outlet for his or her natural talents. She feels very content with who she is and with what she has done with her life. However, she has based her sense of well-being primarily on what she has done. Because she discovered her talents and found a profitable and prestigious way of using them, all seems well for the moment.

But all it takes is a small freak accident, a divorce, a hit-and-run, a child who is harmed, and Claire's world could turn upside down. All the rewards and the sense of achievement would go out the window. Claire does not realize this since she is still relishing her new triumph over the insecurity and fear of her earlier years. And yet she has read of successful individuals who in the last moments of their life were still wrestling with questions about the purpose of life. Why would they do this? Why would their success not bring them contentment?

Even at this stage in Claire's life, I believe the Creator of the universe patiently waits, asking simply that she give up her attempt to be in control, that she acknowledge that she cannot do it alone and that she doesn't have all the answers. By that simple admission, she would humble herself before God, who knows more and, in fact, created her for a purpose she has only partially discovered.

It seems that the more intellect, the more wealth, or the more status a person has, the more difficult it is for that person to submit to God, the Creator of the universe. Possibly it requires a greater act of humility. In Claire's earlier days at high school or college, she was in danger of being ostracized or laughed at. Then she would have had very little to lose by surrendering her life to God. Now, as an adult with high status and a respectable title, it is easy for her to feel she has too much to lose to risk surrender to the unknown. That may be why trusting God has always required an act of faith.

Conclusions

As I observe adults who are well into their fifties and beyond, there is often a keen awareness of the finiteness of life. For most of them, the number of their remaining years is substantially fewer than those they have already lived. On the one hand, a lot has happened in the last twenty years; on the other hand, they can remember twenty years ago as though it was last spring. Within twenty more years, they may be gone.

Much to my delight I have met seniors who, having found their natural bent and lived life fully, report rewards in this phase of life: a new source of energy and a new dimension of effectiveness that surpasses any act of the will, self-discipline, education, or preparation. Individuals who have also found a new source of spiritual energy talk about things "flowing out of them." They talk about approaching death without regret for how they have lived or without wondering why they have lived, and they talk about seeing results in life that were far more than they had ever dreamed, results that seemed to happen with hardly any effort at all.

I believe it is never too late to evaluate where you are in your life journey. It is worth the effort to discover the special talents God has placed within you as well as surrendering your life to His calling. There may be risks involved in making changes in your career, lifestyle, or avocation, but those risks will pale in importance as you experience the satisfaction and rewards of employing your gifts and talents in ways that honor the God of the universe.

Epilogue

Navigating the passages of midlife is a bit like navigating a shipping channel. You can't just drift with the tide, or you may end up wrecked on the rocks just under the surface. You need to be alert not only to the direction you want to go, but to the right channel that gives your "boat" enough room to sail smoothly. Along the way you may need to evaluate your position and make course corrections.

Maybe you have seen yourself in one of our five life stories—or a little of yourself in several of them. Some personal evaluation might be helpful while the character's experiences are still fresh in your mind. Here are some questions to get you started:

What phase of adult life do you find yourself in? If, for instance, you are in phase three, try writing a summary of what your experience has been in phases one and two.

What were the factors that affected your decision about what kind of education or training to pursue?

How would you describe your occupational experience thus far?

What areas of your life give you the most satisfaction? The least satisfaction? Do you know why?

Look beyond your "occupation." What activities or relationships give you the most satisfaction? The least satisfaction? Do you know why?

Even if you feel fairly satisfied with what you are doing in life at this point, it can be highly beneficial to discover and understand more about your natural talents, to guide you as you face new crossroads and decisions along the way. (This is important not only when evaluating various job options that might open up in the future, but also in deciding how to invest your free time or evaluate requests for your volunteer help—at church, your kids' school, or local community organizations.) Appendix A provides a talent definition summary to help you determine what your natural talents are.

Appendix B includes some of my observations about the nature of institutions and the way the world turns. I believe they're important to know for successful navigation of the midlife passage in the world of work.

Finally, I encourage you to share your thoughts and any questions this book has raised with your spouse, a few trusted friends, even a pastor or occupational counselor. Feedback from several sources can be helpful: How do others see you? What do they think are your talent strengths (and nonstrengths)? Where do they see you using your natural talents in the most productive way? Brainstorm ideas with them regarding ways you might employ your talents more productively in the future.

Throughout our journey together in this book, I have attempted to go beyond my observations of men's and women's lives and have also inserted references regarding my belief in a supreme Creator who, out of His infinite wisdom, chose to endow each of us with natural aptitudes by an act of His will. I do not presume that you, the reader, need to agree with my position of faith in order to benefit from the insights contained in this book. On the other hand, if you are at a passage juncture in life and are struggling with a lot of questions, I want to be quick to say that correctly identifying your aptitudes and aligning them with a challenging work opportunity and lifestyle can still leave an empty gnawing inside for meaning and purpose in the latter part of life.

I would be amiss not to present my position as clearly as possible: There is, I believe, a supernatural level of existence for which we are created, and the shallowness of this life journey merely frustrates each of us and motivates us to go beyond. Yet, as we grope to reach out to something more, it is the manner in which we reach out that will either bring eventual success or continued frustration.

In my understanding of the God of the universe as revealed through the Holy Bible, until we finite individuals totally surrender ourselves, our vision, and purpose for our lives to Him, we have not qualified ourselves to enter into that supernatural arena. This is not a statement of knowledge on my part, but one of faith and understanding as I have made the study of the Holy Scriptures part of my life quest. Further, in order for mankind to comprehend the infinite vastness of a supernatural power, God provided a living example of Himself for a time during the history of the world. According to the scriptural record, that representative is the Christ, the God-man Jesus, who walked on this earth for thirty-three years. A person who studies the biblical record and seeks to understand this living testimony of the Creator needs to accept Christ as the doorway to relate to God, the Creator of all things.

With this tangible example, we have all that we need to know about the ultimate purpose of life. If we reject this person, Jesus Christ, we consequently reject God, the Creator. This is a very humble position and requires a significant amount of careful thought. It is not a political statement. It is not an initiation rite. It is a point of understanding about life, one's purpose, and one's Creator. Once a person crosses the line of submitting his or her life and purpose to God through Jesus Christ, according to the Scriptures, that person is empowered supernaturally. One is given a second supernatural identity, which in its embryonic form seeks to enable the person to see beyond the physical and material of this world and begin to glimpse the vastness of eternity.

Regardless of how you, the reader, feel about your spiritual dimension, I hope that the content of this journey will be helpful to you as you attempt to reach that goal of master craftsperson.

Best wishes in your life journey.

A P P E N D I X

A

Talent Definitions Summary

To help you gain a better understanding of natural talents, I have defined fifty-four of them below. As you review these talent definitions, keep in mind that each represents an inherent aptitude, not a learned skill acquired through on-the-job training or formal instruction.

I. Communication

Communication refers to the aptitude for relating thoughts, feelings, and ideas. Each person has at least one and a maximum of three of the predominant modes of communication from the fifteen listed below.

1. Writing

The natural talent for clearly conveying information, moods, or feelings through the use of written words.

You may have this talent if you
- are good at communicating through writing
- find that writing comes naturally to you

2. Conversing

The natural talent for generating and sustaining an easy flow of one-to-one discussion resulting in a sense of mutual understanding.

You may have this talent if you
- communicate well one-on-one with others
- find that talking with another person is your most effective means of communication

3. Public Speaking

The natural talent for persuasively and accurately presenting information, moods, or feelings through the use of the spoken word targeted to a live audience. (See also #15, Giving Presentations.)

You may have this talent if you
- find that speaking is one of your most effective means of communicating
- you can get your point across when speaking before an audience with limited interruptions

4. Teaching

The natural talent for presenting information in an easily understandable way to a group. The emphasis is on audience understanding. (See also #13, Moderating, and #15, Giving Presentations.)

You may have this talent if you
- have a knack for making a complex subject easily understood by others
- find that people learn quickly when you are teaching

5. Broadcasting

The natural talent for conveying information, moods, or feelings through verbal discussion using the telephone, video broadcasting, radio broadcasting, or other audio-visual media.

You may have this talent if you
- feel comfortable when communicating through electronic media
- are very effective communicating over the telephone

6. Designing

The natural talent for expressing moods, ideas, or concepts through design layout including graphic arts, architecture, drafting, landscape drawing, and so forth.

You may have this talent if you
- are good at conceptualizing an idea through the use of lines and drawings
- have a good grasp of artistic design

7. Painting

The natural talent for expressing moods, feelings, or concepts through painting with oils, pastels, chalk, and so forth; does not necessarily include detailed design.

You may have this talent if you
- are good at expressing a mood or feeling through painting
- find that your paintings give others a certain new insight to life

8. Colors and Patterns

The natural talent for expressing moods or feelings through the arrangement of colors, patterns, fabrics, or textures such as in clothing, wallpaper, photography, or silk screening.

You may have this talent if you
- have a knack for expressing thoughts and feelings through colors and patterns
- have a knack for spotting right color combinations in most any situation

9. Shapes and Forms

The natural talent for expressing moods or feelings through the arrangement of objects, shapes, or undefined forms, including room arrangement, architectural landscaping, housing or urban planning, and sculpture. Does not necessarily include space or cost efficiency. (See #20, Order of Your Space.)

You may have this talent if you
- have a knack for understanding how objects and shapes affect people's moods and feelings in the layout of a room, the floor plan of a house, or the design of a neighborhood
- are particularly adept at sculpturing wood or clay objects

10. Handicrafts

The natural talent for expressing a mood or feeling through the creation of jewelry or other craft items made of wood, leather, cloth, or other materials.

You may have this talent if you
- are good at expressing a mood or feeling through making of crafts
- are adept at crocheting, knitting, and other cloth or fabric crafts

11. Music

The natural talent for expressing a mood or feeling through music via written composition. This talent is not necessarily associated with performing talents (#12–15) or Creating talent (#21).

You may have this talent if you
- convey your thoughts and feelings most accurately through music
- find that people get a better understanding of themselves, life, and their feelings when they hear your music

12. Acting

The natural talent for modifying one's behavior and attitudes to portray a defined character.

You may have this talent if you
- have a knack for portraying a character other than yourself
- are good at performing in front of others
- are good at cross-cultural encounters when you try to imitate those around you

13. Moderating

The natural talent for facilitating group discussion or group interaction. Talent is normally exercised while standing or seated in front of a group.

You may have this talent if you
- have a knack for leading group discussions
- feel very comfortable in helping those who are reluctant to speak in a group to express their thoughts

14. Singing or Instrument Playing

The natural talent for performing before an audience through the means of singing or instrument playing, which does not necessarily require a music-composing talent. (See #11, Music.)

You may have this talent if you
- express yourself in a way that words cannot convey when singing or playing your instrument
- find that when performing musically, something comes over you that allows you to express yourself better than any other way you know

15. Giving Presentations

The natural talent for giving presentations in front of others that include audience interaction such as management briefings, workshops, seminars, giving announcements, or performing the role of a master of ceremonies.

You may have this talent if you
- are at your best up in front of others giving presentations
- are able to think on your feet while interacting with an audience

II. Relationships

A second category of aptitude concerns relating to others. Everyone has at least one most effective relational capacity.

16. MultiRelational

The natural talent for quickly establishing rapport with all types of people on first encounters. Repeated contact generally does not enhance effectiveness of initial contacts. This talent is displayed one-on-one or with a group; does not necessarily include public speaking (#3).

You may have this talent if
- meeting new people comes easily for you
- you adjust easily to the differences in new relationships

17. Familiar-Group Relational

The natural talent for developing rapport with an established group of individuals through repeated contact. Continued interaction generally increases relational bonds.

You may have this talent if you
- are usually at your best in a friendship after you've gotten to know someone over a period of time
- prefer to work in an environment where you see the same people over and over

18. Singular Relational

The natural talent for working on a project by oneself or with two or three other people over an extended period of time. Because of limited interaction with the public, relationships with friends are usually very deep and long lasting. This talent does not exclude casual interaction within the public arena; nor does it exclude Public Speaking (#3) or Teaching (#4) talents.

You may have this talent if you
- work best when you can concentrate all of your attention on a particular project without being interrupted by others
- work best when you have a few individuals to relate to that you have known for a long period of time

III. Functional Capacities

A third category represents one's task-oriented behavioral aptitudes. Each person has at least three to five out of the thirty-six as strengths.

19. Time and Priorities

The natural talent for ordering one's own schedule to reflect what is the most important task at any given time and how long it will take; does not necessarily include the ability to order time and priorities for others. (See #25, Planning.)

You may have this talent if you
- set personal priorities (and make adjustments) quickly and easily
- always seem to get the important things done on time

20. Order of Your Space

The natural talent for ordering one's personal space (i.e., closet, desk, shelves, files) for sensing the most efficient positioning of materials for easy retrieval, and for maintaining things in their proper place. Does not necessarily include the ability to order space for others. (See also #49, Classifying.)

You may have this talent if you
- always seem to have a need to put things in their proper place
- have a strength in keeping things organized

21. Creating

The natural talent for forming new associations among previously unrelated concepts, objects, or systems. It likes to continually experiment or tinker with new ideas. This talent can be observed in cooking (new combinations of foods) and teaching (new visual aids), as well as advertising (new market approaches); does not necessarily require much knowledge of previously developed methods or resources.

You may have this talent if you
- are always coming up with new ideas on how to do things
- are a very creative person

22. Imagining

The natural talent for forming new associations in one's mind through theorizing, philosophizing, daydreaming, hypothesizing, developing story characters, and so forth.

You may have this talent if you
- have a vivid imagination
- find yourself part of a different world that you create in your mind

23. Inventing

The natural talent for development of new technical equipment and/or electrical systems, and also developments in wood, concrete, plastic, or glass.

You may have this talent if you
- have a knack for inventing
- have a knack for coming up with better ways to improve machinery and equipment and how they function

24. Developing/Initiating

The natural talent for envisioning new goals (what needs to be done) for a group of people such as a church, department, or company. Talent includes the capacity to motivate others to accept the goals and to initially oversee the start-up efforts to accomplish them. This is not to be confused with the character trait of being a self-starter or the persuasive talents (#37–39), as these do not necessarily include the capacity to be responsible for others.

You may have this talent if you
- are good at motivating others to start up new projects or programs
- are usually referred to as an entrepreneur

25. Planning

The natural talent for projecting one's thinking into the future to determine the details and sequence of events: resources needed, potential problems, reserves necessary for emergencies, and hidden costs, as related to a group project; does not necessarily include organizing time and personal space talents (#19, 20), which relate only to one's personal schedule.

You may have this talent if you
- have a knack for mapping out the step-by-step details to accomplish an organizational long-term goal
- are talented in planning out the details for organizational objectives

26. Managing

The natural talent for coordinating the efforts and activities of others in achieving a common goal. Includes the capacity for encouraging each individual to make his or her maximum contribution. Talent prefers a stable, established work environment.

You may have this talent if you
- have a knack for managing the individual efforts of others to achieve a common goal
- find that your style of management is easy to follow and brings out the best in others

27. Physical Coordination

The natural talent for overall physical activity including use of arms, body, and legs in a skillful, coordinated fashion; talent is not limited to sports activities; may include some vigorous physical activities.

You may have this talent if you
- are athletically coordinated
- seem to have a knack for skillfully coordinating your body, arms, hands, and legs in vigorous physical activity

28. Hand-Arm Coordination

The natural talent for physical activity including use of one's hands and arms in a coordinated fashion. Talent is most often expressed in skillful use of tools while repairing, assembling, sewing, hammering nails, and so forth.

You may have this talent if you
- have a knack for using your hands and arms in a coordinated way
- are good at using your hands and arms as in repairing, building, or constructing projects

29. Operating or Driving

The natural talent for skillfully coordinating pedals, levers, typewriter keys, office machines, steering wheels, or gear shifts, simultaneously so as to effectively run equipment, machinery, helicopters, automobiles, and so forth.

You may have this talent if you
- have a knack for driving vehicles
- have a knack for operating most types of equipment and machinery

30. Hand-Fingers Coordination

The natural talent for precise, detailed physical activity including use of one's hands and fingers in a skillful, coordinated fashion. Talent is expressed in use of small tools, precision assembly, detail painting, and so forth.

You may have this talent if you
- have a knack for precision detail work
- are highly dexterous in using your hands and fingers in working with precision tools and equipment

31. Tutoring

The natural talent for assisting others one-on-one in overcoming learning problems or disabilities.

You may have this talent if you
- have a knack for helping others overcome learning problems
- seem to be effective when working one-on-one to help another with a disability

32. Being of Service

The natural talent for helping others to achieve their goals and meet their needs.

You may have this talent if you
- seem to be able to come alongside and help others get their goals accomplished
- like to help people get ahead with their projects

33. Counseling

The natural talent for sensitively evaluating individual needs, desires, or dreams; does not necessarily include detailed presentation of realistic solutions. Knowledge of detailed solutions is normally dependent on proper training and education.

You may have this talent if you
- have a knack for helping people work through their problems
- are adept at counseling others

34. Reassuring and Supporting

The natural talent for individually empathizing with another's hurts, frustrations, or anxieties. It should result in comfort and support, not necessarily provide solutions to problems.

You may have this talent if you
- have a knack for encouraging others when they are down
- like to come alongside people and lift them up

35. Discerning Character

The natural talent for discerning people's character quickly and accurately.

You may have this talent if you
- usually read people pretty well
- find people rarely fool you

36. Projecting into the Future

The natural talent for predicting future trends, opinions, or fads, as related to international politics, popular clothing styles, or social and cultural trends.

You may have this talent if you
- have a knack for sensing the outcome of certain events like elections or opinion surveys
- can usually tell what is coming down the road in terms of popular opinion

37. Negotiating

The natural talent for grasping the needs and/or desires of at least two unrelated persons or groups, finding a common denominator in both and uniting all in the agreement of a defined goal, idea, or product.

You may have this talent if you
- have a knack for settling disputes between others
- usually can see both sides to an argument and then bring both to a consensus

38. Selling

The natural talent for introducing a concept or object in a manner acceptable to an individual or group so as to result in a sale. Talent is also applicable to recruiting volunteers.

You may have this talent if you
- are good at closing deals
- seem to be good at recruiting others to commit themselves

39. Promoting

The natural talent for directly or indirectly motivating another's thoughts or behavior towards acceptance of a subject matter, opinion, or persons.

You may have this talent if you
- find that when you are excited about something you usually will get several others to feel the same way
- are a natural promoter, always looking for something to tell others about

40. Physical Environment

The natural talent for noticing visual detail in one's surroundings.

You may have this talent if you
- notice small things that others often miss
- find that others tell you that you see much more of life's details than they do

41. Printed Documents

The natural talent for noticing visual detail in blueprints, maps, legal documents, technical manuals, and so forth. Talent may include manuscript-editing ability.

You may have this talent if you
- have a knack for proofreading
- cannot stop your eyes from noticing details in printed documents, blueprints, or manuscripts

42. Spatial Perception

The natural talent for seeing a three-dimensional object or building from a two-dimensional drawing. Talent is usually demonstrated when reading mechanical drawings, blueprints, maps, or aerial photographs.

You may have this talent if you
- can see a completed building from a blueprint
- find that when you look at a dress pattern you can normally see the finished dress

43. Calculating

The natural talent for quickly and accurately performing numerical computations such as percentages, arithmetic functions, or statistical probabilities; may also include accounting and bookkeeping.

You may have this talent if you
- are good with math
- are aware that working with numbers has always come easily for you

44. Recording

The natural talent for counting and recording individual items and/or numerical values in a precise, accurate manner; may also include accounting and bookkeeping.

You may have this talent if you
- have a knack for counting and recording items
- are very thorough in counting and recording inventory, numbers, or information

45. Troubleshooting

The natural talent for discovering the source of a mechanical/electrical/technical failure or breakdown. One's approach may appear as spontaneous or more step-by-step; does not necessarily include the ability to use tools in the repair of technical failure, or the ability to propose a detailed solution. Knowledge of a detailed solution is normally dependent on proper training and education.

You may have this talent if you
- have a knack for diagnosing technical problems
- have a knack for troubleshooting mechanical problems

46. Problem Solving

The natural talent for discovering the source of an error (human logic). One's approach may be either spontaneous or systematic. Talent does not necessarily include the ability to propose a detailed solution, which is normally dependent on proper training and education. (See also #33, Counseling.)

You may have this talent if you
- enjoy figuring out the strategy to resolve a problem
- find that others tell you that you are able to get to the root issue of a problem quickly

47. Researching/Investigating

The natural talent for seeking, gathering, or probing for information concerning a certain subject matter or object. Talent is not limited to reviewing literary or computer information resources but may include interviewing and telephoning people.

You may have this talent if you
- have a knack for thoroughly gathering information about a particular subject
- are good at interviewing others to find out what they know about a certain subject

48. Remembering

The natural ability to tally, record, and quickly recall details.

You may have this talent if you
- have a knack for remembering details
- remember people's names without any problem

49. Classifying

The natural talent for efficiently classifying information so it can be retrieved easily.

You may have this talent if you
- have a knack for efficiently classifying information
- are a whiz at filing and maintaining information storage

50. Analyzing

The natural talent for examining, dissecting, or contemplating a given concept, subject matter, or object in order to understand its component parts and interrelationships. Talent is more curious to know things than driven to find solutions to problems. (See #46, Problem Solving.)

You may have this talent if you
- often feel driven to completely understand a concept, philosophy, truth, or physical law
- love to examine something to understand why it is the way it is

51. Evaluating/Appraising

The natural talent for appraising the monetary value of almost anything or judging the feasibility of a proposed idea, business venture, or new product. May also include the ability to appraise or judge the value of completed projects, business ventures, and so forth. Does not necessarily include Planning (#25), Future Projection (#36), or Problem Solving (#46) talents.

You may have this talent if you
- have a knack for knowing what something is worth
- can usually spot a good buy

52. Synthesizing

The natural talent for examining ideas, elements, or concepts in order to bring them together to form a whole.

You may have this talent if you
- have a knack for gathering different opinions on a subject and bringing them all together
- are a natural synthesizer

53. Being Decisive

The natural talent for quickly reacting to an immediate emergency and making a fast, responsible decision. Talent is usually a physical response as in paramedic, athletic, referee, military, and other applications. Talent differs from Evaluating and Appraising (#51), primarily in the quickness of response.

You may have this talent if you
- have a quick reflex when encountering emergency situations.
- seem to react quickly to unexpected moves while playing sports

54. Taking Risks

The natural talent for being productive where the successful outcome of future programs, investments, or expenditures is unknown.

You may have this talent if you
- have a knack for moving ahead when there is only a 50/50 chance of succeeding
- find that the chance of losing everything you have doesn't hold you back if the cause is worthy

Reflections for Your Journey through the Five Phases

As I have observed people in a wide variety professions, as well as the organizations where they work, I have gained some insights that should be helpful regardless of your natural talents or occupation.

1. How You Want Others to See You

In most employment situations, if you don't teach others how to understand what you do best, they will impose their standards on you. This could be simply demonstrated in an office potluck where the labor is being shared: A person could either volunteer to do something because he or she is gifted in a particular way or wait until someone else assigns him or her a task because nobody wants to do it.

Your career advancement is most likely affected by evaluations of your work performance. This should give you the opportunity to discuss your talent strengths with your employer. If you are not aware of a formal process for evaluating your productivity, consider asking your employer to perform an annual evaluation to clarify the employer's expectations and identify how you are using your strengths.

2. The Need Versus the Vacancy

If you want to accomplish something in life, look for unmet needs rather than identified vacancies or job openings. Look for what is not currently being accomplished, a problem unsolved, a goal not yet attained. The hottest opportunities exist where the person in charge makes a decision to solve a problem but hasn't yet decided how to do it.

Most people go through life looking for job vacancies that have already been defined and structured (the salary, the job duties, the desk, the office) rather than seeking out new or expanding companies that might need people even though they haven't yet listed any job vacancies.

3. The "Management" of Organizations

If a company or organization (profit or nonprofit) is going to survive long-term, it must have three talents represented at the top: the Initiating talent (#24), the Planning talent (#25), and the Managing talent (#26). Those are found to be mutually exclusive talents. If a person has one, he or she will most likely not have the others. Normally, this does not mean that an effective company or organization must have these three talents embodied in three different people simultaneously.

Usually the founder sets the tone: Even if he or she died years ago, the spark and enthusiasm of that Initiating talent is still alive in the company. Now the Managing talent is taking over, trying to make it more profitable and efficient, or the Planning talent is coming in and making a contribution for the future.

The behavioral characteristics of the Initiating talent can be impulsive, shooting from the hip, and they usually get things going right away. They are not afraid of dramatic change. The Managing talent is much more stable: a company led by a person with Managing talent usually experiences slow, sustained growth. The Planning talent is usually laid-back, not hasty to give an opinion until all the facts are clearly presented.

4. Advancing to the Ideal Job

Eighty percent of American businesses have twenty or fewer employees. This means that the majority of companies tend not to be highly structured. As an organization grows and attempts to become more efficient and profitable, however, it gets more organized to the point where every job description has a number and a detailed explanation of what the job is and how it works. This needs to happen in order for a large company to survive and remain effective; but in the process it sometimes will become so structured that the creativity that is so critical to its success will be stifled or forced out.

Also, because a high degree of structure is efficient, it is viewed as the model or standard of the way things should be. In fact, it is these large corporations that are featured in *Business Week* and *Forbes* and are taught as examples at graduate business colleges. Therefore, people who want to succeed get in their mind that they must get on the elevator at the bottom floor and the way to get ahead is to please the elevator operator.

Sometimes the ideal job is discovered by identifying a problem in a smaller company that is giving the owner a headache—a problem that can be solved by using your natural talents.

5. When Considering a Change

Usually, if a person has achieved a certain leadership position or other "recognized" measure of stature such as a doctoral degree, a job change becomes a sensitive issue. I have found that even severe stress is not enough to cause change. As long as one faces leaving a known problem without tangible hope for something better, the pain of the present is preferred. Time needs to be taken to explore new career fields while still employed in the present position. Once a new goal is identified and found to be realistic, letting go of the old pain is far easier. This principle has helped many voluntarily quit secure but painful jobs for new challenges.

6. Education

In educational settings, a certain amount of knowledge must be transmitted from the teacher to the student. For mature students (older than high school), I believe it is the students' responsibility to learn all they can from the instructor; they set the standard they are going to live with. If the instructor's abilities are limited, the student should move on and get knowledge elsewhere.

In a mature student's mind, this transition to self-directed learning can occur in high school, though it normally does not happen until college or graduate school. Until it happens, the student thinks, "If I get an A in class, I have mastered the subject matter and have mastered that part of life." The irony is that the professor may not have mastered that aspect of life and therefore what is taught in class may not apply to life. Sometimes the standards for academic knowledge are different from those for career mastery.

7. The Reward of Labor

In reading the Bible, the Book of Ecclesiastes places a superior value on the pursuit of labor and the mastering of a craft, not necessarily the attainment of some goal or award (the blue ribbon, the gold cup). The person who has a craft and enjoys doing it well is highly esteemed and called blessed. In a lifetime such a person reaches a certain status where he or she is viewed as a master craftsperson—not necessarily the best in his or her field, but certainly respectable and a contributor to society. This is not necessarily the same as trying to climb to the top of the ladder and become the president or the highest-paid person.

8. The Image of Leadership

As a rule of thumb, people tend to listen to the most visible person in an organization. If the figurehead—the person out front—is not the person in charge, there will be confusion among the followers. There are extenuating circumstances where variations can be negotiated, but they are rare and require constant education: "If you have this need, go to this person, but if you have a different need, go to someone else." Even then, the arrangement is so contrary to human expectation, that the organization may lack focus and forward movement.

9. The Will Versus the Emotions

People tend to follow a style of decision making based either on feelings or facts. Their personalities and talents predispose them to one style or the other. For example, those who are more emotional, artistic, or creative are inclined to buy a car based on how it feels when they sit behind the wheel, how it looks, and the prestige and status that it brings. Those with stronger talents in Order of Space and Numerical Calculating and an objective personality bent will choose their cars based more on things like its gas mileage, price, and resale value.

In life, some decisions should be made with the emotions, and others should be made by evaluating the facts. What throws the switch between an emotional or factual decision is the will. Part of the maturing process is learning to exercise that will contrary to our temperament's inclination—for instance, when the emotions are screaming to take over (I'm desperate; I have to get one of those; I'm afraid), the will takes over to calm the fervor of the moment so that reason prevails.

Decisions that are better based on the emotions are selection of music, the color of a room, landscaping a yard, and selection of a vacation site, a hobby, a pastime, a movie, a book to read, a cake, a steak, or a restaurant. Decisions that should be based on facts are the purchase of a refrigerator or an automobile, a job, when to have children, when to get married, or what college to attend.

10. Nonstrengths versus Weaknesses

You should never consider your talent nonstrengths as weaknesses. Nonstrengths are inherent limitations. Weaknesses are personality characteristics that should be changed.

Everyone has weaknesses, such as losing one's temper, being judgmental, being domineering, and being impulsive. I believe that a person who has submitted his or her life to God receives the Holy Spirit, who matures and refines him or her. Theologians call this process sanctification, which works like a rock tumbler to smooth and remove the rough edges that inhibit spiritual growth. The Spirit of God can do far more than we mortals can when it comes to growing spiritually.

Talent nonstrengths are very different. They, like our talent strengths, are inherent qualities God has bestowed on each of us. An example is a person who is tone deaf. It can't be changed. Most things are not so absolute; our nonstrengths are usually just things we can't do well. But they are limitations, and I believe they are God-given. He does not expect us to eliminate them or be ashamed of them. Therefore, they do not weaken us in fully serving God as He intends.

Only two things related to our talent strengths or nonstrengths can hinder us in living to our full potential: not knowing what our strengths and nonstrengths are (and thereby attempting tasks we're ill equipped to do) and failure to surrender one's life to God.

11. Nonstrengths and American Individualism

If our nonstrengths are not weaknesses to be corrected so we can be well-rounded, maturing people, then how do we live with the obvious deficiencies they represent?

This question arises out of a kind of individualism that presumes each person ought to be able to do everything well. It's based on that myth of human omnipotence articulated by Napoleon Hill: "Whatever the mind conceives and the heart believes, I can achieve." If we are so capable, we should pull ourselves up by our own bootstraps and quit burdening our neighbor with our inadequacies.

The Bible's answer to this is interdependency. We are created to need others. In the Christian vernacular, that is called the Body of Christ—the church—where each person's unique talents and gifts are recognized as well as each person's nonstrengths and therefore the need for other members of the body. For the rest of our lives we will be dependent on others because we never will be the best at everything.

12. Nonstrengths and Basic Adequacy

Acknowledgement of our nonstrengths does not excuse irresponsible behavior in the areas of our limitations. A person needs to be adequate even in the areas of nonstrength. Just because it is hard to accomplish something in a nonstrength area doesn't mean we should avoid it. If a person takes a job that includes some tasks in areas of his or her nonstrengths (and every job will), that doesn't give the person license to be irresponsible in those areas. He or she may have to work doubly hard just to do an adequate job or need to obtain extra training in order to do those things in even a passable way.

Remember the 60/40 principle. No job will be free of the "drudgery" tasks in areas of your nonstrengths, but if you can keep them down to about 40 percent, you will be able to soar in the areas where you can shine. If that 40 percent uses up a disproportionate amount of your energy, as it probably will if you perform those tasks adequately, you should not be surprised.

13. The Pursuit of Excellence

The fact that you cannot add a talent or eliminate a nonstrength does not mean that your talents are static in their effectiveness. You can and should develop and improve your talents. The best analogy is that of an athlete or musician. Just because a person has everything it takes to make a good showing in a local track meet or talent show doesn't mean he or she is going to compete in the Olympic Games or perform at the New York Metropolitan Opera unless discipline and hard work hone and polish those aptitudes. If it is possible for a disciplined person with a B or B+ aptitude to outperform an undisciplined person with an A+ aptitude, isn't that an encouragement for us to identify our A+ strengths and then apply that diligence and pursuit of excellence in those areas?

14. Setting Life Goals

Most people who set life goals make the goals first and then seek ways to accomplish them. A better alternative, especially for career planning, is to assess your talent resources and set your goals accordingly.

This means more than looking at your current occupation or schooling and saying, "Well, what can I accomplish? What is available to me? What can a math major do? What can a salesperson do?" That limits you to your current circumstances. In order to accomplish this alternative thinking about goals, you need to understand the whole concept of natural talents and how they apply to the world of work. It's not a matter of stepping out on blind faith to conquer the world; it's a very practical analysis of your assets and then a pursuit of an occupation that allows you to feature those strengths.

15. When One Plus One Equals Three

Whenever a president, CEO, or senior pastor develops a trust-bond relationship between himself or herself and a subordinate such that they have mutual respect and a solid working relationship, the actual productivity of the two individuals equals the output of three full-time people. This multiplication factor can also apply for multiple subordinates.

Why is this true? Normally, in executive and upper-management circles, a large percentage of time is spent compensating for hostility, conflict, and stress that is caused by incompatible work relationships. This kind of stress is debilitating. It undermines confidence. A lot of time is wasted in protecting one's backside. When people are affirmed and worry less, their productivity increases significantly. They often spend their nonwork hours thinking through issues that apply to their jobs. Their medical bills are less and there is less clock-watching distracting them from their work.

A P P E N D I X

C

About My Passion

Helping People Make a Difference

An NFL football player discovers a new direction for his career. A former pastor gets hired as a Christian college development officer. A nuclear engineer fulfills his lifelong ambition to build yachts. What do these people have in common? They are three of thousands of men and women who have discovered their talents and have been directed to an ideal career niche.

Many folks we counsel at IDAK, the midcareer-transition company I founded in 1980, have a genuine passion for making a difference with their lives and want to use their abilities to the fullest. Too many feel like throwing in the towel because they haven't found their proper niche, the area of work where their natural talents can be best used.

The meaning of IDAK is "unique identity." ID comes from the word "identity" and AK is taken from a Hebrew derivative, meaning "unique" or "uniqueness." We are headquartered in Portland, Oregon, but also have licensed offices in other major metropolitan areas throughout the United States.

At IDAK, our unique midcareer transition service combines personalized counseling with state-of-the-art technology. We use a three-part, in-depth career-assessment and job-transition service to assist a person in getting hired in the ideal career position.

Although the initial assessment provides an extensive evaluation and matching of a person's aptitudes to career options, it isn't until each individual experiences getting hired for the ideal opportunity that the true realization of his or her full potential becomes believable.

I find it so rewarding to watch executives, reentry homemakers, pastors, teachers, and others finally learn where they function best. They're normally more effective once they are able to release their talents into the area of work that suits them.

If you have questions about your natural talents and career growth, feel free to contact us: IDAK Group, Inc.,7931 N.E. Halsey, Suite 309, Portland, OR 97213, phone (503) 252–3495.